GRAYBEARD
★ LECTURES ★

Hope With Its Sleeves Rolled-Up

Philanthropy That Leads to Action

from the Whiteboard of
Mark "Dr. Maddog" Donnelly, PhD.

RPSS PUBLISHING – BUFFALO, NEW YORK

drmaddog@hotmail.com

The Graybeard Lectures - Hope With Its Sleeves Rolled-Up

Perfect Bound ISBN: 978-1-956688-73-3

Printed in the United States of America

10 9 8 7 6 5 4 3 2 1

RPSS Publishing - Buffalo, New York

Hope, left alone, politely waits in the
corner with its fingers crossed.

But in your hands,
in your decisions, your words,
and your work, it rolls-up its sleeves
to make a difference.

TABLE OF CONTENTS

Introduction - Behind Every Donor is a Reason -7

Part I –The Old Lies We Tell Ourselves - 13

Chapter 1 - The Organization Is Not the Hero -13

Chapter 2- Information Is Not Persuasion -17

Chapter 3- Awareness Is Not Impact -21

Part II –The Donor as Protagonist -25

Chapter 4 - Casting the Hero -25

Chapter 5 - The Offer –A Chance to Matter -29

Chapter 6 - The Stakes Must Be Real -33

Part III –The Machinery of Emotion -37

Chapter 7- Feeling First, Thinking Second -37

Chapter 8 - The Power of One -41

Chapter 9 - Clarity Is Mercy -44

Part IV –Structure, Strategy, and Discipline -47

Chapter 10 - The Repeatable System -47

Chapter 11 - Measurement Without Losing Your Soul -51

Chapter 12 - The Long Road No One Sees – Why Basic Research Matters -55

Chapter 13 - Scaling Trust, Not Just Revenue -60

Part V –Trust: The Only Currency That Matters -64

Chapter 14 - The Long Memory of Donors -64

Chapter 15 - Proof Is the Promise Kept -68

Chapter 16 - Gratitude That Isn't Transactional -71

Part VI –The Ask -74

Chapter 17 - Asking Is an Act of Respect -74

Chapter 18- Timing, Tone, and Tension - 77

Chapter 19 - The Second Gift Is the Real Test -81

Part VII –The Whole System -85

Chapter 20 - The Bridge Model -85

Chapter 21 - Corporate Philanthropy -89

Chapter 22 - What This Looks Like in the Wild -95

Chapter 23 - A Few Things Learned the Hard Way -99

Bibliography -104

About the Author -107

BEHIND EVERY DONOR IS A REASON

There are two kinds of rooms in philanthropy.

The first is easy to recognize.

It is bright. Confident. Full of charts and clean lines. Someone stands at the front with a laser pointer, explaining a strategy that sounds inevitable if everyone simply follows the plan. Words like engagement, conversion, and optimization drift through the air, precise and well-placed, like tools laid out on a table.

Everything appears in order.

Everything appears solvable.

And yet, there is another room.

Quieter.

You might not notice it at first, but it is where the work actually lives. A kitchen table late at night. A hospital waiting area where time moves differently. A lab humming with fluorescent light, where the experiment is not cooperating. A desk with a blank page and a sentence that refuses to come together.

In that room, no one is presenting.

They are wrestling.

With a question that does not fit neatly into a slide or a strategy deck:

How do you turn hope into something that actually moves?

This book belongs to that room.

Because hope, left alone, is a fragile thing.

It waits. It wishes. It sits still, polite and well-intentioned. But the kind of hope that changes outcomes—the kind that builds institutions, funds research, carries people through uncertainty—does not behave that way.

It rolls up its sleeves.

It shows up early, before the outcome is clear.

It stays when the work becomes difficult to explain.

It continues without the guarantee that it will succeed.

That is the kind of hope philanthropy is built on.

And it is the kind of hope this work depends on.

Over time, a pattern becomes difficult to ignore.

Most organizations are doing meaningful work.

And many of them struggle to explain that work in a way that invites someone else into it.

They produce reports when what is needed is a story.

They present need when what is needed is purpose.

They speak about themselves when they should be making room for someone else.

And the result is predictable.

The response is polite. Thin. Forgettable.

Not because the work lacks value.

Because the value was never made visible in a way someone could step into.

This is where the misunderstanding begins.

Marketing, in many organizations, is treated as something secondary. A bridge between intention and funding. A necessary function, but not the work itself.

That view does not hold.

At its best, this work is not persuasion.

It is invitation.

You are not asking someone to admire what you do.

You are asking them to take part in something that matters—and to see clearly where their decision, their effort, their contribution becomes part of the outcome.

Hope, in this sense, is not a feeling.

It is a role.

Strip everything else away—the tools, the platforms, the shifting language—and what remains is simple.

People give because they want their hope to do something.

To build.

To change.

To prevent.

To discover.

They want to know that what they chose to support made a difference that would not have happened without them.

Not someday.

Now.

Your job is not to impress them.

Your job is to show them where their hope can go to work.

As you move through this work, you will notice certain ideas returning.

That is not repetition for its own sake.

It is because the fundamentals are not complicated.

They are simply easy to overlook.

The donor is not the audience. They are the one who acts.

Clarity outperforms cleverness more often than we would like to admit.

Emotion opens the door. Trust keeps it open.

Proof is how hope learns it was not misplaced.

Everything else is secondary.

There is something else worth understanding early.

This work does not always reward you immediately.

You can tell the story well and still wait.

You can build something thoughtful and watch it move slowly.

You can do everything with care and still wonder, at times, whether it is enough.

Stay with it.

Because when it works—when someone sees the opportunity, understands their place in it, and chooses to step forward—it does not feel like marketing.

It feels like movement.

Hope deciding not to sit still.

This becomes even more apparent in basic research.

You are not offering a finished answer.

You are offering the beginning of one.

A question.

An idea.

A possibility that may take years to unfold.

That is not easy to communicate.

But it is where every meaningful discovery begins.

And if you can show someone how their support moves that first step forward—how their decision becomes part of the process, not just the outcome—you are no longer asking them to wait.

You are asking them to participate.

There is, throughout this work, a certain skepticism.

Not of hope itself—but of how casually it is often used.

Hope is not a slogan.

It is not decoration.

It is not something placed at the end of a message like a finishing touch.

Hope is a commitment.

And when it is paired with clarity, honesty, and proof, it becomes something more durable than optimism.

It becomes work.

Work that matters.

So this is where we begin.

Not with tactics.

Not with templates.

Not with the idea that this can be reduced to a checklist.

We begin with a shift.

Away from describing.

Toward doing.

Away from observation.

Toward participation.

Away from passive hope–

and toward hope with its sleeves rolled up.

Pull up a chair.

There's work to be done.

CHAPTER ONE

The Organization Is Not the Hero
(Or, How Good Work Learns to Get Out of Its Own Way)

There is a certain tone that settles over organizations with time. It is not exactly arrogance. It is something quieter and more ordinary than that: habit. A kind of institutional gravity begins to take hold, tugging every sentence, every appeal, every presentation back toward the same center. We did this. We built that. We have achieved these things. On the surface, it sounds reasonable. Even proper. After all, those things are true. The organization did build, accomplish, and serve. But the trouble begins the moment those truths take over the story. When the organization becomes the hero, the donor slips quietly out of it. Not with indignation. Not with resistance. They simply drift out of frame.

This is why so much nonprofit messaging feels less like an invitation and more like a résumé recited aloud. It lists years of service, programs delivered, people served, awards received. Every point may be accurate. Every point may be respectable. But respectability is not the same thing as persuasion. A résumé is built to answer one question: Why should you choose us? Philanthropy is built on another entirely: Why should this matter to me? Those are not neighboring questions. They belong to different conversations. One places the institution at the center. The other places the reader there. Only one of them leads naturally to action.

Anyone who has worked in this field has seen what happens next. An organization does meaningful work. The mission is real. The need is plain. The people involved are capable, committed, often exceptional. A campaign goes out into the world and the response comes back decent enough to avoid embarrassment, but thin enough to disappoint. A few gifts arrive. Some people engage. There is enough interest to suggest approval, but not enough to suggest urgency. Then comes the usual diagnosis: we just need to get this in front of more people. But reach is rarely the true problem. More often, the message has asked people merely to observe, not to enter.

That is the invisible wall organizations build without meaning to. When they tell their story entirely from the inside out, they create distance. Not rejection. Not hostility. Just distance. The donor becomes an audience member, a reader, a spectator to something worthy. But not a participant in it. And people do not fund what they only watch from the sidelines. They fund what they feel connected to.

That is why the real work begins not with a new platform or a new campaign, but with a change in orientation. The message has to move from "Here is what we are doing" to "Here is what becomes possible because of you." It sounds like a modest shift, almost grammatical. It is not. It changes the center of gravity. The story no longer asks the donor to admire the work from afar. It asks them to recognize their place inside it.

Because that is the quiet question beneath almost every donor's reading, whether they ever say it aloud or not. Where do I fit in this? They are not primarily wondering how impressive the organization is, how long it has existed, or how many people already support it. They are wondering whether their stepping in will alter anything at all. If your message leaves that question unanswered, the donor is left to guess. And when people have to guess, they usually decide not to act.

The difficulty, of course, is that this is harder than it sounds. If it were merely a matter of changing a few pronouns, the problem would have been solved long ago. But organizations are inward-facing by necessity. They must think in terms of staffing, budgets, programs, outcomes, logistics, deadlines, and systems. Donors do not live inside those structures. They think in terms of meaning. They want to know what matters, why it matters, and how their action changes the picture. Bridging that gap requires more than editing. It requires translation.

And translation is not the same thing as simplification. The goal is not to flatten the work until it becomes vague or sentimental. The goal is not to make the work smaller. It is to make the point of entry clearer. You are not reducing the truth. You are making it accessible enough for someone outside the institution to enter it.

The difference becomes obvious in practice. An organization-centered sentence might say, "Our institute is conducting groundbreaking research in cellular biology to better understand disease mechanisms." There is nothing false in that sentence. It is accurate, informed, even impressive. But it is distant. A donor-centered version says, "We are working to understand why healthy cells begin to fail and how to stop disease before it starts. Your support helps move that discovery forward." The work has not changed. The science has not changed. Only the center has changed. One version describes. The other invites.

There is often a quiet fear beneath this shift, and it is worth naming. Some organizations worry that if they stop placing themselves at the center of the story, they will somehow diminish their own credibility. In practice, the opposite happens. The work becomes more compelling, not less, because it is no longer occupied with insisting on its own importance. It is showing what can actually be done, and who can help do it.

Making that shift requires discipline. You will always be tempted to add another detail, another credential, another achievement, another paragraph of explanation. Much of it may be valuable. That is not the point. The point is that value is not the same thing as movement. What moves someone to act is not always the fullest possible explanation. It is often the clearest one. And clarity demands restraint, which can feel uncomfortably like leaving good material on the cutting-room floor.

A useful test is simple enough to ask before any message leaves your desk: Is the donor clearly inside this story, or are they still standing outside it? If they remain on the outside, the draft is not finished. The revision needed is not about tone or style so much as position. The work is to keep adjusting until the donor can see, almost without effort, where they belong.

That principle sits beneath everything else: the organization is not the hero. The donor is the one who acts. The institution has an important role, of course. It builds the frame, tends the work, holds the expertise, keeps the lights on, and makes the mission possible. But its role is not to stand at the center of the story. Its role is to light the path clearly enough that someone else can step forward.

Because, in the end, organizations do not move missions forward by themselves. People do. Organizations organize that movement, sustain it, and give it shape. But the act that changes things, the decision to give, to support, to enter the story, always belongs to a person. And if your story does not leave room for that person, then no matter how worthy the work may be, it will remain politely and quietly outside their reach.

In the next chapter, the next comfortable illusion comes apart: the belief that if people simply understood more, they would give more. It is an appealing thought. It is also, much of the time, wrong.

Chapter Two

Information Is Not Persuasion

(Or, Why Knowing More Rarely Leads to Giving More)

There is a belief that takes hold early in this work and lingers far longer than it should. It sounds reasonable when you first hear it. It even feels fair. If people really understood what we do, they would support us. It has the ring of common sense. And like many things that sound like common sense, it is only partly true.

That is what makes it so difficult to shake. If it were entirely wrong, it would collapse quickly. Instead, it stays just plausible enough to keep people working very hard in the wrong direction.

When a campaign underperforms, the response is almost predictable. The assumption is not that something fundamental is off, but that something is missing. More explanation, perhaps. More detail. A clearer description of the complexity involved. So the next version grows. It adds context, then background, then supporting data, then clarification of the data. Each revision feels more complete than the last.

And yet the results rarely change in any meaningful way.

Because the problem was never that people lacked information. The problem was that information was never the thing that moved them in the first place.

People like to believe they make decisions by weighing facts and arriving at a conclusion. In reality, the process is less orderly. Something catches their attention. Something creates a feeling. A decision begins to take shape. Only then does logic arrive to explain why that decision makes sense. By the time information is doing its work, the direction is already set. Or it isn't.

This is the quiet truth underneath so much of this work: people do not give because they understand. They give because something in them responds. Understanding can support that response. It can reinforce it. It can give it structure and confidence. But it cannot replace it. You can explain a problem with precision and depth and still leave people unmoved. You can tell a simple, clear story and watch people act with very little additional information. That is not a flaw in the audience. It is how people are built.

Information, for all its value, carries a cost. Every additional sentence asks for attention. Every layer of complexity demands effort. And effort is where many messages quietly fail. Not because they are inaccurate. Not because they are poorly intentioned. Because they ask too much of someone who has not yet decided to care.

You have seen this play out. An appeal opens with context, then stretches into background, then deepens into data, then pauses to explain the data. By the time it reaches the point–the reason it exists at all–the reader has already begun to drift. Not out of indifference. Out of fatigue.

This is the difference between reporting and moving. Reports exist to capture everything that is true. They need detail. They depend on completeness. Fundraising is something else entirely. It is not a record of activity. It is an invitation to act. And those are not the same task.

The contrast becomes clear in even the simplest example. You can say, "Each year, over six million individuals are affected by this condition. Our organization has developed multiple programmatic responses…" It is accurate. It is thorough. It is also inert. Or you can say, "Every day, people who were healthy begin to lose control of their own bodies. We are working to understand why–and how to stop it. You can help move that work forward." The amount of information decreases. The likelihood of movement increases.

This does not mean information has no role. It does. But it is not the engine. It is the support beam. Once someone is engaged–once they feel that something matters–information becomes useful. It answers the questions that follow: Is this real? Is it credible? Do these people know what they are doing? But it only works after the door has been opened. If you lead with it, you are asking it to do a job it was never designed to do.

Organizations fall into this pattern for understandable reasons. They know the work deeply. They live inside it. They see its complexity, its nuance, its interdependencies. They feel a responsibility to convey that depth accurately. That instinct is honorable. It is also, if left unchecked, counterproductive. Because what feels like necessary explanation from the inside often feels like unnecessary effort from the outside.

This is where translation becomes essential. Not simplification for its own sake, but translation with purpose. Your role is not to transfer everything you know. It is to carry across what matters. To take something complex and render it in a way that can be grasped quickly, felt immediately, and acted upon without hesitation. You are not shrinking the truth. You are making it usable.

A useful constraint is to try to explain your work in ten seconds. Not every detail. Not every nuance. Just the core. What is happening, why it matters, and what can be done. If that cannot be done clearly, adding more information will not solve the problem. It will only make it harder to see.

Simplicity, in this context, is often misunderstood. It is not the absence of intelligence. It is the result of discipline. To say something clearly, without excess, requires judgment. It requires restraint. It requires a willingness to leave things out. And that is where most people hesitate, because leaving something out feels like risk.

But the greater risk is not saying too little. It is saying so much that nothing lands.

There is always a moment, early in any message, when the reader decides whether to continue. It comes quickly, faster than most organizations design for. If that moment is filled with information, then information is carrying the weight of that decision. It rarely succeeds. What carries that moment is something else entirely.

That is why a better question to ask before sending any message is not what the reader will learn, or even what they will understand, but what they will feel in the first few seconds. If the answer is unclear, distant, or neutral, the message will likely follow the same path.

The principle is simple, but it takes discipline to apply: information supports action. It does not create it. Lead with what moves. Support with what proves.

There is nothing wrong with wanting people to understand your work. But understanding is not the goal. Action is. And action does not begin with something tidy and well-ordered like information.

It begins with a feeling.

In the next chapter, we will take apart a belief that sits right beside this one, and often reinforces it: that if more people were simply aware of your work, more people would support it. It sounds obvious. It is, more often than not, misleading.

Chapter Three

Awareness Is Not Impact

(Or, Why Being Seen Is Not the Same as Being Supported)

There is a particular comfort in being noticed.

You can see it in the numbers. Impressions rise. Views climb. Clicks accumulate. Followers gather. The graphs move in the right direction, and for a moment, it feels like progress. The activity is visible, measurable, easy to report. It gives you something to point to, something that suggests forward motion.

But beneath that sense of movement sits a quieter question, one that rarely receives the same attention.

Did anything actually change?

Not how many people saw the message. Not how many heard about the work. But whether anyone chose to act.

Because in philanthropy, awareness is not the finish line. At best, it is the front gate.

Awareness is seductive precisely because it can be measured so easily. It produces numbers that look good in reports. It creates a sense of accountability, of traction, of momentum. And in environments where results are expected and scrutinized, something that can be counted begins to feel like something that counts.

But visibility and impact are not the same thing. They are not even close.

You have likely seen the pattern before. An organization invests in a campaign. Reach expands. Engagement ticks upward. The audience grows. There is a sense, briefly, that things are working. Then the campaign ends, and the numbers that matter most come into view. Gifts. Retention. Ongoing support.

And the change is modest. Sometimes barely there.

This is where awareness reveals its limitation. It can open a door. It cannot make someone walk through it.

Part of the reason this pattern persists is that awareness allows organizations to stay busy. There is always something to post, something to share, something to amplify. It creates motion, and motion feels productive. But motion and progress are not the same thing. A campaign can generate considerable activity and still produce very little movement.

Between awareness and action, there is a gap. Not a technical gap, but a human one. It is the distance between seeing something and deciding that it matters. Between noticing and participating. Most organizations invest heavily in the first step. Far fewer spend time understanding the second.

When results fall short, the instinct is almost automatic. The answer must be more. More reach. More impressions. More exposure. More visibility. But if the message does not move the people already seeing it, expanding the audience simply multiplies the same outcome. A weak message does not become stronger when it is amplified. It becomes louder.

This is where the distinction between attention and engagement begins to matter. Attention is passive. It happens to someone. They scroll, glance, briefly register that something exists. Engagement requires more. It requires interest, relevance, a reason to stay. But even engagement is not the goal. Someone can read, click, even share–and still choose not to act.

What is missing is meaning.

The shift from "I've heard of this" to "This matters to me" is the moment everything changes. Without that shift, awareness remains surface-level. It creates familiarity, and familiarity can lead to comfort, but neither guarantees commitment.

Consider the difference between two statements. Thousands of people saw our campaign. Someone decided to give because of it. Only one of those changes anything.

This is not to say that awareness has no value. It does. People cannot act on what they have never encountered. But awareness is a beginning, not an outcome. Its worth is determined entirely by what follows it.

Which means the more useful question is not how to get more people to see the message, but what happens immediately after they do. Is there a clear next step? Is the message strong enough to hold attention once it is captured? Is the invitation unmistakable? If those elements are missing, awareness dissipates. It does not convert itself.

When organizations place too much emphasis on awareness, something subtle begins to shift. They start optimizing for visibility, for shareability, for surface-level engagement. And in doing so, they drift away from the things that actually produce results–clarity, emotional connection, meaningful action. The mission does not change, but the focus does.

A growing audience can feel like progress. It suggests potential. And potential has value. But potential, on its own, does not fund anything. It does not advance research. It does not sustain programs. It waits.

A better measure is quieter, and often less impressive at first glance. Not how many people were reached, but how many people moved. Who gave. Who responded. Who stayed connected. Who took a step beyond observation.

These numbers are smaller.

They are also the only ones that matter.

The difference becomes clear even in the language we use. "Help us spread the word" asks for amplification. It keeps the audience at a distance. "You can help move this work forward today" offers a role. It invites participation. One extends the message outward. The other brings someone into it.

This is where discipline comes in. Every message should have a purpose beyond being seen. Not simply to inform broadly or increase general visibility, but to prompt a specific action, to create a specific response. If that purpose is unclear, the message drifts. And so do the results.

The principle is straightforward, even if it is often overlooked: awareness creates opportunity. Action creates impact. Confusing the two leads to a great deal of activity with very little change.

It is entirely possible to be widely known and poorly supported. To be frequently seen and rarely acted upon. To succeed at awareness and still fail at impact.

Because the work is not to be noticed.

The work is to matter—and to make that mattering clear enough that someone chooses to do something about it.

In the next chapter, the focus shifts. Away from what does not work, and toward what does. It begins with a simple, and often uncomfortable, change in perspective: seeing the donor not as an observer, but as the one the story has been waiting for.

CHAPTER FOUR

Casting the Hero

(The Quiet Art of Letting Someone Else Step Into the Story)

Every story has a center.

Not a topic. Not a theme. A person.

Someone who faces something, decides something, and does something. Remove that person, and what remains is not a story at all. It is a description–accurate, perhaps, but static. Nothing moves because no one is there to move it.

Organizations, by their nature, tend to drift toward that center. They build the work. They manage the effort. They understand the complexity in ways others do not. And so, when it comes time to tell the story, they stand where they have always stood–in the middle of it.

It feels natural. It also quietly breaks the story.

Because when you occupy the central role, there is nowhere left for anyone else to go.

When a donor encounters your message, they are not looking for a performance. They are not there to admire the work from a distance. They are looking, whether they realize it or not, for a place. A way in. Some indication that if they step forward, something will shift because they did.

If that role is not clearly available, they do not object. They do not push back. They simply remain where they are.

This is the difference between an audience and an actor. An audience observes. They watch, they listen, they may even admire. But they do not change the outcome. An actor, even in a small role, alters the direction of the story. They take part. They matter.

Your donor does not want to sit in the audience, even if they never say it out loud.

Making this shift introduces a quiet tension. If the donor becomes the central figure, what happens to the organization? Does it fade into the background? Does it lose importance?

No. It becomes something more useful.

The organization becomes the guide.

The one who understands the terrain, who knows what is at stake, who can show the path forward. It holds the knowledge, the tools, the structure that make the work possible. But it is not the one who takes the step.

This is not a lesser role. It is the role that makes the story work.

Beneath every effective fundraising message, whether it is consciously structured this way or not, there is a pattern. There is a problem or a possibility. There is someone who can act. There is a path forward. And there is an outcome that depends on that action.

When the organization places itself in the position of the one who acts, the structure collapses. The reader is left without a role, and without a role, there is no movement.

This shift often begins with something that seems almost trivial: language. A sentence like "We are leading innovative research to address…" centers the organization as the actor. A sentence like "You can help move research forward that aims to…" opens space for someone else.

The difference is not grammatical. It is structural.

People respond to the sense of agency—that their decision carries weight, that their action changes something, that their participation matters. Without that, even a compelling message can feel distant. Interesting, perhaps. Worthy, even. But not urgent.

Some organizations attempt this shift halfway. They include the donor, but keep themselves firmly at the center. "With your help, we will continue our important work…" It sounds collaborative, but it still places the donor in a supporting role.

The distinction is subtle. The effect is not.

Compare that with a cleaner frame: "Your gift will help uncover why healthy cells begin to fail–and how to stop it." Now the donor is not supporting the action. They are part of it.

This is what the reader is quietly trying to understand as they move through your message. Not through formal analysis, but through a kind of internal sense-making: If I do this, what happens? If the answer is vague, abstract, or buried beneath organizational language, the process stalls. If it is clear, immediate, and tangible, the next step becomes easier.

There is always a temptation to hold on to the center. To maintain control of the narrative. To ensure the organization is fully represented. But control, in this case, comes at a cost. Stories that are already full leave no room for participation. And people do not step into spaces where there is no place for them.

So the work becomes something different. Not adding more, but making room. Space for a decision. Space for an action. Space for someone to recognize themselves in the outcome.

That space does not appear by accident. It has to be created.

A simple exercise can make this visible. Take a recent message and look at the verbs. Who is doing them? Who is making things happen? Who changes the outcome? If the answer is consistently "we," then the story is still centered in the wrong place. Revise until "you" carries real weight–not as decoration, but as action.

And something else happens when you step back from the center. The work itself becomes clearer. It is no longer competing with your presence in the story. It becomes the path, the context, the structure that makes action possible.

The principle is simple, but it is not optional. The donor is not supporting the story. The donor is the one who moves it forward. Everything else must align around that.

Because stories do not move simply because they are told well. They move because someone inside them decides to act.

Your job is not to be that someone.

Your job is to make it unmistakably clear who that someone can be—

and to leave just enough space for them to step into it.

In the next chapter, we turn to what that step actually represents. Not funding. Not support.

Something far more compelling:

A chance to matter.

CHAPTER FIVE

The Offer –A Chance to Matter

What You're Really Asking For When You Ask for Money

Let's set something aside at the outset.

You are not asking for money.

At least, not in the way most people think about it.

What you are actually asking for is something far more personal. You are asking someone to take a piece of themselves–their time, their attention, their resources, their intention–and place it into a future that does not yet exist. Money is simply the form that decision takes.

This distinction matters more than it first appears, because most fundraising language misses it entirely. It treats the gift as the point. "Please donate." "Support our work." "Make a contribution." These are instructions. They describe the action. But they leave the meaning behind that action largely unspoken. And without meaning, the action carries very little weight.

When someone considers giving, they are not evaluating your spreadsheets. They are not reviewing your internal plans. They are making a quieter calculation, one that has less to do with information and more to do with significance. Does this matter enough for me to step in? If I say yes, does it count for something?

That is the question sitting underneath the decision.

Because money, in this context, is not just a resource. It is a signal. A way of saying this matters, I want to be part of it, I am choosing this over something else. When the ask is framed purely as a transaction, that signal gets flattened. Something meaningful is reduced to something mechanical.

Every fundraising message, whether it is carefully constructed or hastily assembled, contains an offer. It may not be stated clearly. It may not even be intentional. But it is there. And the strength of that offer determines what happens next.

A weak offer tends to sound like this: help us continue our important work. It is polite. It is respectable. It is also indistinct. It asks for support without giving the reader anything concrete to step into. A stronger offer sounds different. Help uncover why healthy cells begin to fail–and how to stop disease before it starts. Now there is something specific. Something that can be pictured. Something that can be chosen.

This is where many organizations default to need. They explain what is lacking, what is required, what is at risk. And while need is real, it is rarely what moves people on its own. Opportunity does. Need says we are missing something. Opportunity says you can make something happen. That shift–from absence to possibility–is where movement begins.

At its simplest, people want their actions to matter. Not in a vague or symbolic way, but in a way that can be understood and, if necessary, pointed to. Because I did this, something changed. If your message does not make that connection clear, it is asking for effort without offering meaning.

A common weakness appears here. Organizations describe their work thoroughly. They explain what they do, how they do it, and why it is important. But they leave one question unanswered: what changes because of me? The omission is rarely intentional. But it has consequences.

Reframing the message changes very little about the work itself, but it changes everything about how it is received. "We are expanding our research initiatives to better understand disease progression" becomes "You can help accelerate research that aims to stop disease before it takes hold." The work is the same. The offer is not.

Clarity matters here. Vague offers produce vague responses. "Make a difference" is a sentiment. It gestures in the right direction, but it gives no clear sense of what that difference is. "Help fund the next step in understanding how this disease begins" provides direction. It gives the reader something to grasp, something to step into.

There is often hesitation at this point. A concern that being too direct will feel too forceful. Too forward. So the language softens. It becomes indirect, implied rather than stated. But hesitation in the ask creates hesitation in the response. If you are unclear about what is being offered, the donor cannot be clear about what they are deciding.

Clarity, in this sense, is not aggression. It is respect. It acknowledges that something matters, that the reader has a role, and that it is worth stating plainly. Indirect language shifts the burden to the reader, asking them to interpret what is meant. And interpretation is where many decisions quietly dissolve.

Beneath all of this sits something deeper. Every effective offer connects to motivations that already exist. Hope. Concern. Curiosity. The desire to prevent harm. The desire to contribute to something larger than oneself. You are not creating these impulses. You are giving them a direction.

This becomes even more important when the work itself is not immediately visible. Basic research does not offer instant outcomes. It does not provide quick, tangible results. Which makes the offer harder to articulate—and more important to get right. You are not offering a cure. You are offering participation in the discovery that makes cures possible. That distinction has to be made clear.

A simple test can help. Before finalizing any message, ask: what is the donor being invited to do, and why does it matter? If the answer feels vague, it probably is. And if it is vague to you, it will be even more so to someone encountering it for the first time.

The principle underneath all of this is straightforward, even if it is often overlooked. You are not asking for money. You are offering a chance to matter. When that offer is clear, the ask becomes easier to make—and easier to accept. When it is not, no amount of refinement will compensate for the absence.

People do not give because they are told to. They give because something in front of them feels worth stepping toward. Your job is to make that step visible. To show, plainly and without distraction, what becomes possible if they take it—and why it matters that they do.

In the next chapter, we turn to what gives that offer its force. Not information. Not logic. Something more immediate, and more reliable.

Emotion—the quiet engine behind almost every decision.

Chapter Six

The Stakes Must Be Real
Urgency Without Substance Is Just Noise in a Hurry

There is a tone that begins to creep into fundraising when the work feels important.

You can hear it almost immediately. Every message leans forward a little too much, tapping its watch, insisting on its own urgency. Everything becomes critical. Everything becomes unprecedented. Every appeal carries the same refrain: now more than ever, time is running out, we must act immediately.

The intention is clear. The goal is to create urgency.

But more often than not, the effect is something else entirely.

Fatigue.

Because when everything is urgent, nothing is. The language begins to blur. The words lose their weight. And over time, the message loses credibility—not because the work itself lacks importance, but because the language no longer distinguishes between what is truly immediate and what is simply significant.

Donors can feel that difference, even if they cannot quite name it.

This is where it helps to return to what stakes actually are. They are not volume. They are not intensity. They are not how forcefully something is said. Stakes are about consequence. They answer a simple question: what happens if nothing changes? And just as importantly, what becomes possible if it does?

Without clear answers to those questions, a message floats. It may be well-written. It may be thoughtful, even compelling on the surface. But it does not land.

Organizations often try to define stakes in broad terms. They speak of scale. Millions affected. Far-reaching impact. Significant need. These statements are true. But they remain distant. Scale, by itself, does not create connection. People do not respond to numbers alone. They respond to what those numbers mean in real terms.

Bring the stakes down to earth, and the difference becomes clear. Saying that millions are affected by a disease communicates size. Saying that someone who was healthy last year can suddenly lose the ability to move, speak, or think clearly communicates reality. The facts are the same. The weight is not.

There is a temptation, when trying to create urgency, to stretch the language. To heighten the moment just a little beyond what is strictly true. To lean into intensity in the hope that it will prompt action.

It rarely works for long.

Not because donors immediately reject it, but because they gradually stop trusting it. Trust is not lost in a single moment. It erodes quietly, over time, as the gap between what is said and what is felt widens.

Real stakes do not need to be inflated. They need to be specific. They show what is at risk, who is affected, and how it unfolds. They do not rely on generalities. They do not assume importance. They demonstrate it.

The difference can be subtle, but it is decisive. "We are at a critical turning point in our mission" announces importance. It tells the reader how to feel. "Without new support, this line of research will slow—delaying answers that could change how this disease is treated" explains consequence. It allows the reader to see what is at stake.

Urgency, when it is real, does not need to shout. It is simply clarity about timing. Why this moment matters. What is happening now that will not remain the same later. It is not panic. It is precision.

And not every message needs it.

Some work is inherently long-term. Foundational. Slow by necessity. Forcing urgency into those messages creates a kind of friction that people can sense. It feels off, even if they cannot explain why. It is often more effective to say plainly that the work takes time–but cannot move forward without support–than to manufacture a deadline that does not exist.

This becomes especially important in basic research, where outcomes are not immediate and certainty is not guaranteed. The work is exploratory, incremental, often invisible in its early stages. That makes the stakes harder to articulate, but not less real. They are found not in instant results, but in delay. In missed opportunities. In questions that remain unanswered longer than they should.

You are often describing what has not yet happened. What could happen. What might be prevented. And that requires care. Because possibility, if left vague, feels optional. To make it real, it must be tied to consequence. Without this work, we remain in the dark about why this disease begins. Now the absence itself becomes visible.

From the donor's perspective, none of this is theoretical. They are not analyzing your language. They are evaluating your reality. Is this truly important? Does timing matter? Is my action meaningful now, or can it wait?

If your message does not answer those questions clearly, the default answer is almost always the same: it can wait.

And waiting, in this work, often becomes not acting at all.

This is where discipline matters. The discipline to resist exaggeration. To avoid overstatement. To rely not on borrowed urgency, but on what is actually true. Even if it feels quieter. Even if it requires more precision. Because truth, clearly stated, carries more weight than urgency that is merely asserted.

A simple test can help. Ask yourself what specifically is at risk if nothing changes. Then ask what specifically becomes possible if it does. If those answers are unclear, the stakes are not yet defined.

And without clear stakes, there is nothing to move toward–or away from.

The principle is straightforward: stakes are not declared. They are demonstrated. Show the consequence, and urgency will follow on its own.

Because people do not act simply because something is labeled important. They act because they understand, in concrete terms, what is at risk–and what they can help change.

Your job is not to raise your voice.

It is to sharpen the picture.

Until the stakes are no longer something they are told, but something they can see.

In the next chapter, we turn to what carries that moment forward once the stakes are clear. Not logic. Not detail. Something more immediate, and far more reliable.

Emotion–the quiet engine behind almost every decision.

CHAPTER SEVEN
Feeling First, Thinking Second
The Quiet Order in Which Decisions Actually Happen

There is a version of decision-making people like to believe in.

It is neat, orderly, and reassuring. You gather the facts, weigh the options, reach a conclusion, and then take action. It presents decisions as a kind of clean sequence, guided by reason from beginning to end.

It is also not how most decisions—especially generous ones—actually happen.

The real process is less structured, and far more human. Something catches your attention. Something creates a feeling. A decision begins to take shape. And only then does logic arrive, not to lead, but to explain. By the time the reasoning shows up, the direction is already set. Not completely, perhaps, but enough to matter.

This distinction changes how you approach the work.

If you believe decisions are driven primarily by information, you will design your messages accordingly. You will explain more, justify more, elaborate more. You will build something that feels complete, even thorough. And then you will wonder why the response remains modest.

Because you are speaking to the last step first.

People do not give because they have completed an analysis. They give because something in front of them feels important, immediate, meaningful. That feeling does not replace thought. It comes before it. It answers the first and most essential question: do I care?

Without that, nothing else follows.

Emotion, in this context, is often misunderstood. It is treated as something soft, secondary, less reliable than logic. But emotion is not the opposite of reason. It is the beginning of it. It is what allows reasoning to have a direction in the first place.

And yet many organizations are cautious around it. They worry about being manipulative, about overstating the case, about losing credibility. So they retreat into safer territory—neutral language, measured tone, careful distance. The result is often accurate.

And unmoving.

The problem is not emotion itself. The problem is how it is used. Emotion becomes manipulation when it distorts reality—when it exaggerates, misleads, or reaches beyond what is true. But when it is grounded in reality, it does something entirely different. It clarifies. It shows what something feels like, why it matters, what is at stake in human terms.

That is not manipulation.

That is understanding.

And it does not come from adjectives. Words like urgent, critical, devastating rarely create real feeling. More often, they signal that feeling is being asserted rather than experienced. Emotion lives somewhere else—in specific detail, in human experience, in moments that can be pictured.

There is a difference between saying that a disease is devastating and showing what that means. Someone who was fine yesterday wakes up unable to do something they have always done, without knowing why. The scale may be the same. The impact is not. One tells the reader how to feel. The other allows the feeling to emerge.

There is a kind of restraint required here. The more you try to force emotion, the less effective it becomes. The more you allow it to arise from what is true, the more it resonates. Restraint is not the absence of feeling. It is what makes feeling believable.

Often, emotion enters through something small. Not a sweeping narrative, but a moment. A single image. A contrast between what was and what is. That is enough. It gives the reader something to hold onto, something that makes the abstract real.

Because when someone encounters your message, they are not asking, at least not at first, whether it is logically sound. They are asking something simpler and more immediate: does this reach me?

If the answer is no, the message ends there. If the answer is yes, then logic has something to build on.

This is where information returns, but in a different role. It reassures. It validates. It provides confidence that the response makes sense. But it cannot lead. It can only follow.

Messages that rely entirely on information often feel complete. They contain context, data, explanation. They leave little unsaid. And yet they fail in a quieter way. They offer the reader something to understand, but nothing to respond to.

Neutral language contributes to this. It feels safe. It avoids risk. It maintains a certain professionalism. But it also creates distance. And distance is where action fades.

A useful test is simple. Read your message and ask not what someone would learn, or what they would understand, but what they would feel. If the answer is unclear, the message likely is as well.

This becomes especially important in basic research, where the work itself can feel abstract, technical, removed from everyday experience. The instinct is to explain, to clarify, to make the complexity visible. But even here, emotion is present. It lives in the uncertainty, in the unanswered questions, in the possibility that something fundamental could change.

We are trying to understand why this happens—because without that understanding, we cannot stop it. Now the work has weight. Not because it has been simplified, but because it has been made real.

The principle beneath all of this is consistent. Emotion begins the decision. Logic supports it. When the order is reversed, the message struggles. When it is aligned, everything else becomes easier.

Because you are not asking someone to complete an analysis.

You are asking them to take a step.

And that step does not begin with a spreadsheet. It begins with something quieter. A recognition. A response. A moment when what is in front of them no longer feels distant.

Once that moment exists, the rest of the decision has somewhere to go.

In the next chapter, we narrow the focus even further. Not across broad audiences or categories, but down to something much more precise.

The power of one.

CHAPTER EIGHT

The Power of One

Why One Story Carries More Weight Than a Thousand Statistics

There is a number that shows up again and again in this work.

It is usually large. Thousands served. Millions affected. Entire communities reached. The numbers are meant to carry weight. They signal scale, reach, importance. They look convincing on a page. They read well in a report.

And yet, for all their size, they often land lightly.

Not because they are wrong.

Because they are hard to feel.

When you describe many people at once, something subtle happens. The mind registers the scale, but the connection begins to thin. Large numbers blur. They lose their edges. And without edges, it becomes difficult to hold onto what they mean.

Now shift the frame.

Not many. One.

One person. One moment. One change you can see clearly. Suddenly the picture sharpens. You can imagine it without effort. You can understand it without translation. It no longer feels distant.

The mind can process large numbers. But human response does not work that way. We are built to recognize individuals–faces, moments, specific experiences. One is not smaller than many. It is simply more accessible.

You can feel the difference in even the simplest contrast. Saying that millions are affected informs. It communicates scale. But saying that someone who was healthy last year can no longer walk across a room without assistance–that connects. It brings the reality into focus.

There is often a concern that focusing on one somehow diminishes the larger issue. That it reduces the seriousness of what is happening. In practice, the opposite is true. When you understand one clearly, you begin to understand what is happening to many. Specificity does not shrink the problem. It reveals it.

This is the quiet paradox: the more specific the story, the more widely it resonates. People do not connect to categories. They connect to experiences. And experiences are always individual.

When messages stay too broad, they begin to blend together. Families are struggling. Patients are facing challenges. These statements are accurate, but indistinct. They describe a situation without showing it. They give shape to the issue, but not substance to the experience.

To make something real, you have to narrow the frame. Not forever, but long enough for someone to see it. One moment. One change. One consequence. From there, the larger picture can expand, but it has to begin somewhere concrete.

The difference becomes clear in practice. You can describe a decline in mobility and cognition, or you can show someone struggling to find words they used easily just a year ago. The first explains. The second makes the reality visible.

This requires restraint. The instinct is to include everything, to show the full scope, to make sure nothing is left out. But when everything is included at once, what matters most often gets lost. Clarity comes from choosing what to show first, and trusting that the rest can follow.

Focusing on one does not mean thinking small. It means starting where connection is possible. Once that connection exists, you can widen the lens. This is one story. It represents something larger. But it begins with something that can be seen.

From the donor's perspective, this matters. They are not trying to grasp the full scale of the issue in a single moment. They are looking for something they can understand quickly, something they can feel, something that answers a simple question: what is this, really?

One clear example does that better than a thousand generalized statements.

Even in work that feels distant, like basic research, the principle still holds. The challenge is different, but the solution is the same. The focus may not always be a person. It may be a single cell, a moment where something changes, a question that has not yet been answered. But it is still one point of entry, something small enough to grasp.

Instead of describing complex biological mechanisms, you can describe what changes inside a single cell when it stops functioning the way it should. The scale has not changed. The accessibility has.

A simple test can help. Look at your message and ask whether someone can picture it. Not in general terms, but in specific ones. If they cannot, the frame is still too wide. Narrow it until the image becomes clear.

The principle is straightforward. People do not connect to many. They connect to one. And from that one, they begin to understand the rest.

Large numbers have their place. They can demonstrate reach. They can signal importance. But they rarely move someone on their own.

Movement begins somewhere smaller. Clearer. More precise.

A single point of understanding.

A moment that can be seen.

Something that can be held long enough to matter.

In the next chapter, the focus shifts again—this time to what allows that clarity to hold. Not complexity. Not cleverness.

Something much harder to achieve.

Simplicity that lasts.

Chapter Nine

Clarity Is Mercy

Making Things Easy to Understand Is an Act of Respect

There is a quiet assumption that often goes unchallenged in this work: that complexity signals intelligence.

Longer explanations. More detailed language. More precise terminology. It can feel like rigor. And sometimes, it is. But in communication–especially in philanthropy–complexity more often signals something else entirely.

Unresolved thinking.

Every message you write asks something of the person reading it. Their time. Their attention. Their effort. These are not infinite resources. They are borrowed. And how you use them matters.

When a message is unclear, the burden shifts. It moves from the writer to the reader. Suddenly, they are responsible for making sense of it. They must interpret, translate, piece together what you meant to say. Most will not do that work. Not because they are unwilling, but because they are busy. And when understanding requires effort, attention quietly slips away.

Clarity, then, is not a cosmetic improvement. It is the result of thinking that has been fully worked through. It comes from knowing what matters, removing what does not, and arranging what remains so it can be understood quickly. Clarity is thinking made visible.

This is why it feels difficult.

Writing thoroughly is easy. You include everything you know. You cover every angle. You leave nothing out. It feels responsible. Safe, even. But writing clearly requires something else. It requires choosing one path over many. It requires deciding what to leave behind. It requires giving up the comfort of completeness in exchange for effectiveness.

And that trade is rarely comfortable.

There is a particular illusion in thoroughness. The belief that if everything is explained, nothing is missed. But thoroughness can become a way of avoiding the harder question: what does this actually mean?

You can hear the difference in language. "Our organization utilizes a multifaceted approach to address systemic challenges…" sounds substantial. It feels like something is being said. But it leaves the reader with very little to hold onto. Compare that with something simpler: "We are trying to understand why this problem begins—and how to stop it before it spreads." Fewer words. More meaning.

Clarity is not just about effectiveness. It is also about respect. When you write clearly, you are telling the reader that their time matters. That you will not make them work to understand you. That you are willing to say what needs to be said plainly.

That is not a stylistic choice. It is a posture.

There is, of course, a temptation to be clever. To craft language that impresses, entertains, or stands out. Cleverness has its place. But in fundraising, it often competes with clarity. And when it does, clarity must win. Because cleverness asks the reader to decode. Clarity allows them to understand.

Unclear language carries another risk as well. It does not just confuse. It creates doubt. If a message is difficult to follow, the reader begins to question more than the wording. They begin to question the work itself. Is the impact unclear? Is the organization uncertain? Is this something I should trust? Confusion rarely leads to confidence.

This is why plain language matters. Not because it is simple, but because it is disciplined. It requires you to name things directly, to avoid unnecessary abstraction, to choose words that carry meaning without effort. It is not about lowering the level of communication. It is about raising its effectiveness.

You can see the difference in small shifts. Phrases like "impactful initiatives" or "innovative solutions" sound important, but they drift. Replace them with what is actually happening—what is being done, what will change—and the message settles into something real.

This is especially true in basic research, where clarity is often lost first. The work itself carries technical language that is precise and necessary within the field. But when that language is carried directly into fundraising, it creates distance. "We are investigating protein misfolding pathways" may be accurate, but it is difficult to enter. "We are trying to understand why healthy cells begin to fail" carries the same intent in a way that can be grasped immediately.

Most messages are decided quickly. Not in detail, but in impression. Within a few seconds, the reader determines whether it is worth their attention. Clarity answers that question immediately. Confusion delays it. And delay often leads to exit.

A simple test makes this visible. Read your message and ask whether someone could understand it on the first pass. Not after rereading. Not after careful study. Immediately. If the answer is no, the work is not finished.

Because clarity rarely appears in the first draft. It is shaped through revision. It is refined, reduced, and sharpened. Not by adding more, but by removing what gets in the way.

This is the principle that sits beneath everything that works: clarity is not a style. It is a form of respect.

You are not writing for yourself. You are writing for someone who has no obligation to stay with you. No requirement to finish what you began. No reason, beyond what you provide, to continue reading.

Clarity is what earns that continuation.

It is what allows meaning to land.

And without it, even the most important work can pass by unnoticed—not because it lacked value, but because it was never fully seen.

In the next chapter, the focus shifts from language to structure. From how something is said to how it is built. Because even the clearest message needs a shape that holds.

CHAPTER TEN

The Repeatable System
(Why Good Intentions Need Structure to Survive Contact with Reality)

There is a moment in every organization when someone says, with a mixture of relief and satisfaction, that a campaign worked.

For a brief stretch, that feels like enough. The numbers came in. The response was strong. The effort paid off. And then, almost inevitably, a quieter question follows, one that carries more weight than the first.

Can we do it again?

Not in theory. In practice. With the same constraints, the same deadlines, the same competing demands on time and attention.

Because a single success, no matter how encouraging, is not a system. It is an event.

Most organizations have experienced this. There is always something that worked—a message that landed, a campaign that exceeded expectations, a moment when everything seemed to align. But when asked to repeat it, the explanations tend to dissolve into uncertainty. It came together. The timing was right. We had a strong story that time.

These are not explanations. They are descriptions of luck dressed up as strategy.

Instinct and experience play a role, of course. They always do. But on their own, they do not scale. They cannot be relied upon to produce consistent results under pressure. A system does not replace instinct. It supports it. It creates a structure where good decisions happen regularly, not occasionally.

A system, in this context, is not a rigid process or a script that must be followed step by step. It is a repeatable way of moving from idea to message to action to response without starting from zero each time. It provides a sense of order. What comes first, what follows, what needs to be true before you move forward.

At its simplest, that structure rests on a few essential elements. The message itself–clear, grounded, centered on the donor. The channel–where the message appears and how it is delivered. The cadence–the timing, the sequence, the follow-up that gives the message rhythm. And the action–the specific step you are asking someone to take.

Remove any one of these, and the whole begins to weaken.

There is often resistance to this kind of structure. It can feel restrictive, as though it might limit creativity or make communication mechanical. In practice, the opposite is usually true. When the structure is clear, it frees attention. You are no longer deciding everything at once. You are working within a shape that holds, which allows you to focus on what matters most.

Without that structure, every campaign begins in the same place: uncertainty. What should we say? Where should it go? When should it launch? Each decision stands alone, disconnected from the last. Each step takes longer than it should. And over time, consistency begins to slip.

From the donor's perspective, that inconsistency is not invisible. When tone shifts, when clarity varies, when focus drifts, it becomes harder to understand what the organization represents. A system does not eliminate variation, but it creates coherence. It holds the work together.

At a practical level, the flow is straightforward. First, define the offer. What is the opportunity being presented? Then clarify the stakes. Why does this matter now? Anchor the message in one clear example– something that can be seen and understood. Invite action directly. And then follow through with proof and gratitude, showing what happened because someone chose to act.

None of this is complicated. It is disciplined.

Repetition plays a role here as well, even if it is often avoided. It can feel unnecessary, even redundant, to say the same thing more than once. But clarity does not take hold in a single pass. Most people need to encounter an idea more than once before it settles. A system ensures that the core message is reinforced over time and across channels.

Timing matters more than many realize. A strong message delivered at the wrong moment will underperform. Not because it is weak, but because it was not seen in the right way, at the right time. Cadence answers questions that are easy to overlook: how often is too often, when to follow up, how long to wait. These are not details. They are part of the structure.

A system is not static. It learns. After each campaign, there is an opportunity to ask what worked, what did not, and what should change next time. Not in general terms, but in specific ones. This is how the system strengthens over time.

There is, however, a risk in the other direction. Systems can become too elaborate, too detailed, too rigid. When that happens, they slow the work down instead of supporting it. A useful system should make action easier, not harder. If it becomes burdensome, it needs to be simplified.

This becomes especially important in areas like basic research, where the work itself is complex and requires translation. Without a consistent structure, messages can become uneven—too technical in one place, too vague in another, disconnected from one another entirely. A system keeps the core intact, even as the details shift.

A simple question can reveal whether that structure is in place. If you had to run the same campaign again next month, could you? Not theoretically, but practically. If the answer is uncertain, the system is not yet strong enough.

This is the principle that turns isolated success into something more durable. What works once is an event. What works repeatedly is a system. The goal is not to celebrate the first, but to build toward the second.

Because good work deserves more than occasional success. It deserves consistency. Not perfection, and not identical results every time, but a structure that allows it to be seen, understood, and supported again and again.

In this work, the goal is not a single moment of response. It is sustained movement. And sustained movement requires something steady beneath it.

In the next chapter, the focus turns to how that movement is measured. Not everything that can be counted, but the things that actually matter.

Chapter Eleven

Measurement Without Losing Your Soul
Counting What Matters Without Becoming What You Count

There comes a point in every organization when someone asks a simple question.

How are we doing?

It is a reasonable question. Necessary, even. But it carries a quiet risk—not because it should not be asked, but because of how easily it can be answered.

Numbers step in quickly. They always do.

They offer clarity. They fit neatly into reports. They can be compared over time, arranged into charts, presented as evidence of progress. They create a sense of precision, a feeling that something solid has been captured and understood. In environments where accountability matters, that feeling can be reassuring.

But not everything that can be measured actually matters. And not everything that matters can be measured easily.

When measurement becomes the focus, something subtle begins to shift. The work does not change all at once. It drifts. Incrementally. Quietly. Toward what can be counted instead of what counts.

Messages become shaped for clicks. Content is designed for engagement. Decisions begin to follow the path of what is visible and immediate. And over time, the center moves. Away from meaning, toward measurement.

Some metrics make this easy. They are quick to collect and easy to interpret. Opens, views, impressions, shares. They rise and fall in ways that feel responsive. They offer immediate feedback, which makes them feel important. But what they actually measure is attention, not action.

The numbers that matter most are harder to track. They move more slowly. They require patience. Gifts. Retention. Repeat giving. Long-term engagement. These do not simply tell you how many people noticed. They tell you how many people moved.

The gap between those two sets of numbers can be striking. It is entirely possible to see growth in attention without any meaningful growth in support. More eyes, more clicks, more activity–and at the same time, flat giving, declining retention, limited long-term impact.

This is where interpretation matters. Because the signal is not always where the noise is loudest.

Whatever you measure consistently, you will begin to optimize. Not deliberately at first, but inevitably. If success is defined by engagement rates, the work will bend toward engagement. If success is defined by meaningful support, the work will begin to shape itself around action. The metrics do not just describe the work. They influence it.

Immediate feedback complicates this further. Quick results invite quick reactions. Something performs well, so you repeat it. Something falls short, so you abandon it. But not all impact is immediate. Some messages build slowly. They deepen understanding. They create trust over time. They lead to action later, not sooner.

If everything is judged by short-term response, you risk discarding the very things that create long-term strength.

Philanthropy does not unfold in single moments. It unfolds in patterns. Relationships are built over time, not captured in a single interaction. The more useful questions are slower ones. Do people return? Do they increase their support? Do they stay connected?

These signals take longer to appear. They are also more reliable.

Measurement, then, must be kept in its proper place. It is a tool, not a master. It can inform decisions. It can help you see direction. It can show whether something is landing. But it cannot replace judgment. Numbers can tell you what is happening. They are less reliable in telling you why.

There is a common pattern that illustrates this. An organization notices that a certain type of content performs well. It generates more clicks, more shares, more visible engagement. So they produce more of it. And over time, the content begins to drift. It becomes broader, lighter, easier to consume–and less connected to the work itself.

The metrics remain strong.

The meaning weakens.

When what performs well and what matters most begin to separate, a choice has to be made. Follow the numbers, or correct the course. The easier path is not always the right one. And it often leads away from the mission rather than toward it.

Trust sits at the center of this tension. It does not appear in a single metric. It reveals itself indirectly–in consistent giving, in the willingness to give again, in responsiveness over time. It is built slowly, lost quietly, and difficult to capture in the moment. But it underpins everything else.

This becomes even more complex in basic research, where outcomes are long-term, uncertain, and often invisible in the early stages. You cannot measure success by immediate results alone. Instead, you look for signs of progress, continuity, sustained support. Indicators that the work is moving forward, even if the destination is still out of view.

A useful way to think about this is to separate what you track into two categories. Signals of attention–opens, views, clicks. And signals of action–gifts, retention, repeat engagement. Both have value. But they are not the same, and they should not be confused.

Before reacting to any metric, it helps to pause and ask two questions. What does this actually tell us? And just as important, what does it not tell us? Because every number reveals something, and leaves something else out.

The principle is simple, but it requires discipline to hold onto. Measure what matters. And remember that not everything that matters can be measured quickly.

Numbers are useful. They show patterns, reveal trends, provide feedback.

But they are not the work itself. They are reflections of it.

Your responsibility is not to produce better numbers.

It is to do work that matters—and to measure it in ways that help that work continue, without losing sight of why it exists in the first place.

In the next chapter, the focus shifts again. Not just to growth, but to the kind of growth that holds. Not scaling activity.

Scaling trust.

Chapter Twelve

The Long Road No One Sees
Why Basic Research Matters

Basic research does not begin with an answer.

It begins with a question that refuses to settle.

Something small, often invisible to anyone outside the work. A signal that behaves differently than expected. A pattern that does not quite fit. A moment when what should happen… doesn't. And instead of resolution, there is uncertainty.

That is where the work starts.

And from that point forward, everything about it resists the way most people expect progress to look.

There is no clear finish line waiting just ahead. No immediate transformation that can be pointed to and named. The work moves in increments—quiet, technical, sometimes difficult to explain even to those closest to it. It advances, pauses, redirects, and advances again.

From the outside, it can feel distant.

From the inside, it is anything but.

Which is where the challenge begins.

Because philanthropy, by instinct, looks for something it can see. A result. A change. A before and after that makes the decision feel grounded. Basic research offers something different.

Not a conclusion.

A path.

And that path is longer than most messages are built to hold.

So there is a temptation—understandable, persistent—to shorten it. To compress the timeline. To make the work feel closer to resolution than it is. To suggest that the answer is just ahead, waiting to be reached.

It sounds more compelling that way.

It is also fragile.

Because when the work takes the time it actually requires—and it always does—the gap between what was said and what is experienced begins to widen. Not dramatically. Not all at once. But enough to introduce doubt.

And doubt, once introduced, is difficult to reverse.

The stronger approach is not to shorten the path.

It is to make it visible.

To show what is happening now. Not in its full complexity, but in a way that can be understood without effort. What is being asked. What is being explored. What has shifted, even slightly, because the work continues.

Often, this begins at a scale that feels almost too small to matter.

One cell behaving differently than expected. One signal that does not align. One moment where something begins to change.

These are not outcomes in the way people are used to seeing them.

But they are movement.

And movement is what the donor is supporting.

This is the quiet shift that changes everything.

The donor is not funding a finished result.

They are funding the ability to move forward.

To ask a question that has not yet been answered. To explore a possibility that might otherwise remain closed. To take one step into something that, without support, would remain unknown.

That step matters more than it appears to.

Because without it, nothing else follows.

There is a tendency to focus on where the work will lead. The cure. The application. The moment when everything becomes clear. And those things matter. They are the reason the work continues.

But they are distant.

The donor needs something closer.

What happens now?

What moves forward because this work continues today?

If that can be made clear, the distance to the outcome becomes less of a barrier.

Because the donor is no longer being asked to wait.

They are being asked to begin.

This is where language matters.

Not in how much it says, but in how precisely it holds the truth.

We are working to understand why healthy cells begin to fail.

We are trying to identify what triggers this disease at its earliest stage.

We are exploring what changes before symptoms appear.

These are not conclusions.

They are directions.

And direction, when it is clear, is enough.

It gives someone a place to stand. A point of entry into something that is still unfolding.

The question of proof follows quickly behind.

How do you show that something is working when the work itself is not finished?

The answer is not to wait for completion.

It is to show progress.

What has been learned. What has been ruled out. What is now understood that was not before. These are not endpoints, but they are not nothing. They are evidence that the work is moving.

And movement, when it can be seen, reinforces belief.

Because belief is what carries this work forward.

Not blind optimism, but something steadier. The ability to hold two truths at once. That the work takes time. And that it matters now. That the outcome is not immediate. And that the progress is real.

This kind of patience is not automatic.

It has to be built.

Through clarity. Through consistency. Through showing, again and again, that something is happening–even when that something is still incomplete.

The timeline cannot be shortened.

But the path to participation can.

The ask must meet the donor where they are.

Help fund the next step.

Support the work being done right now.

Not someday.

Now.

Because the donor does not need to see the end.

They need to see where they enter.

And once they enter, something else begins.

The relationship.

Basic research depends on continuation. The work extends. The questions deepen. The answers take time. Which means the first gift is not the point. It is the beginning of something that must hold.

That holding depends on what follows.

Not just reporting, but translation. Showing what has moved, and how that movement connects back to the decision that made it possible.

Without that, the work drifts out of view.

With it, the donor remains part of the process.

And that is the real shift.

They are no longer observing the work.

They are inside it.

There is a discipline required here.

To resist overstating. To avoid promising certainty where there is none. To speak plainly about what is not yet known, while showing what is being done to understand it.

Uncertainty, in this work, is not a weakness.

It is the beginning of discovery.

And when it is communicated honestly, it builds a different kind of trust. One that can hold over time. One that does not depend on immediate results to remain intact.

Because what is being offered is not speed.

It is participation.

The chance to be present at the beginning of something that does not yet have a name. To support the step before the breakthrough. To take part in the work that makes everything else possible.

There is no shortcut through that.

No way to make it immediate without losing what makes it true.

But there is a way to make it clear.

To show what is happening now.

To connect it to what becomes possible later.

To invite someone into the process, not just the outcome.

And when that happens—when someone sees the work, understands where they fit, and chooses to step in—they are not waiting for change.

They are part of what makes it happen.

Chapter Thirteen

Scaling Trust, Not Just Revenue
Why Growth That Weakens Belief Is Not Growth at All

There is a moment in this work when things begin to move.

The response improves. Gifts increase. Attention grows. The effort starts to feel like it is working, not just in theory, but in practice. And with that momentum comes a natural question, one that feels both necessary and promising.

How do we scale this?

It is the right question. It is also the point where many organizations begin, almost without noticing, to drift.

The first instinct is predictable. Growth appears, and the response is to amplify. Reach more people. Send more messages. Increase the frequency. Expand into new channels. More in, more out, more everywhere.

And for a time, it can work.

Until something quieter begins to shift.

The message broadens just slightly. The tone adjusts to accommodate a wider audience. The clarity softens to feel more inclusive, more flexible, more universal. Each change is small enough to seem harmless. But taken together, they begin to erode the very thing that made the work effective in the first place.

Trust.

Because growth is not simply an increase in volume. It is an expansion of relationship. More people understanding the work. More people believing in it. More people choosing to stay connected over time. Without those elements, growth becomes shallow. It spreads outward, but it does not hold.

This is where the distinction between reach and depth begins to matter. Reach tells you how many people encountered the work. Depth tells you how many stayed with it. Both have value, but they are not equal. A large audience with little commitment is fragile. A smaller audience built on trust is durable.

Trust, once established, has a compounding effect. It builds slowly—one clear message, one honest interaction, one fulfilled promise at a time. But over time, it begins to reinforce itself. Donors return. Giving deepens. Relationships strengthen. Growth built on trust sustains itself. Growth built only on attention must be rebuilt again and again.

As organizations grow, there is often pressure to make the message more universal. To smooth out its edges, to broaden its appeal, to make it resonate with as many people as possible. The language becomes safer, more inclusive, less precise.

And less effective.

Because it is specificity that creates connection.

When a message is stretched to reach everyone, it often ends up fitting no one particularly well. It becomes general, interchangeable, easy to overlook. In trying to reach more people, it loses the ability to move anyone deeply.

A better approach is not to broaden the message, but to repeat it. Not mechanically, but consistently. To allow more people to encounter the same clear, focused idea. Clarity scales. Confusion multiplies.

This is where structure becomes essential. A repeatable system ensures that as the volume increases, the message remains consistent, the tone stays grounded, and the core ideas do not drift. Without that structure, growth introduces variation. And variation, over time, introduces inconsistency.

Growth, then, is not just about expansion. It also requires restraint. Knowing what not to change. What to protect. What must remain intact even as everything else increases.

There is a familiar pattern that illustrates the risk. An organization begins to grow. They experiment with new messages, new formats, new angles. Some work. Some do not. Over time, the original clarity becomes just one version among many. The message does not disappear, but it loses its central place. And with that, its strength begins to fade.

Maintaining the center becomes the work. Returning, again and again, to the core questions: What are we offering? Why does it matter? How does someone take part? As long as those remain clear, growth strengthens the work. When they begin to blur, growth starts to dilute it.

This becomes even more delicate in areas like basic research, where the work is already complex, long-term, and difficult to translate. As you scale, the temptation to simplify increases—to make the message easier, quicker, more immediately appealing. But oversimplification carries its own cost. It can weaken credibility, erode trust, and misrepresent the work itself.

The goal is not to make the work smaller.

It is to keep it clear.

A simple question can help anchor this: as we grow, are we making this clearer, or just louder? If the answer is louder, something needs to be adjusted. Because volume does not create trust. Clarity does.

Trust depends on consistency. Consistency of message, of tone, of follow-through. Growth places pressure on all three, which is why they must be actively protected.

The principle that emerges from this is straightforward, even if it requires discipline to follow: scale what builds trust, not just what increases volume. Growth without trust is temporary. Growth built on trust endures.

It is easy to measure growth in numbers. Harder to measure it in belief. But belief is what sustains the work. It is what brings people back. What deepens commitment. What turns a single act into an ongoing relationship.

If you protect that–if you scale with it, rather than around it–you build something that can hold.

In the next chapter, the focus shifts again. Away from strategy and systems, toward something quieter and more fundamental.

Trust itself.

CHAPTER FOURTEEN

The Long Memory of Donors
What You Do After the Gift Matters More Than What You Did Before It

There is a moment every organization works toward.

The gift arrives. The campaign converts. The appeal lands. A decision is made.

It feels like an ending.

It is not.

It is the beginning of something far more fragile.

What happens next is often treated as routine. The message is sent. The acknowledgment goes out. The system records the transaction. And then attention shifts forward–to the next campaign, the next appeal, the next goal.

But the donor does not experience it that way.

For them, something just happened. They made a choice. They took a step. They entered the story. And now, whether they realize it consciously or not, they are waiting to understand what that step meant.

This is where the real work begins.

Donors remember less than we assume, and more than we expect. They may not recall the exact language of the appeal, or the structure of the message, or the details that felt so carefully constructed at the time. But they will remember how it felt to give. What happened afterward. Whether the connection they stepped into held, or quietly dissolved.

Those impressions form quickly.

And they last.

Every gift carries with it an unspoken question. Not about the amount, or the mechanics of the transaction, but about meaning. Was that worth it? Did it matter? Did anything change because I chose to act?

The answer to that question is not found in the appeal. It is found in what follows.

When stewardship is thin, the consequences are rarely immediate. There is no dramatic failure. No moment that clearly signals something has gone wrong. Instead, the shift is gradual. Enthusiasm softens. Connection fades. The next ask feels slightly less compelling. And over time, the relationship begins to thin.

Not because the donor changed.

Because the experience did.

If the interaction ends with the gift, it becomes a transaction. You asked. They gave. The exchange is complete. But philanthropy is not sustained by transactions. It is sustained by relationships. And relationships do not end at the moment of action. They deepen there—or they begin to fade.

Donors do not notice everything. But they notice enough. Whether they were thanked promptly. Whether the acknowledgment felt real. Whether they heard what happened because of their gift. Whether they are remembered as more than a line in a database.

These are small moments.

They carry disproportionate weight.

There is a difference, for instance, between acknowledgment and gratitude. An acknowledgment confirms that something was received. A transaction completed. Thank you for your gift. Gratitude does something more. It connects the action to meaning. Because of you, this work moves forward. The first closes the loop. The second extends it.

Every appeal makes a promise, whether it states it explicitly or not. It suggests that the work matters, that action will lead to something meaningful. Follow-through is where that promise is either strengthened or weakened. Updates, progress, visible movement–these do not need to be dramatic. They need to be real.

Trust is not created in the moment of the ask. It is reinforced afterward. Through consistency, honesty, and clarity over time. Each interaction adds to it, or takes something away. Rarely in a single moment. Almost always gradually.

One of the most common patterns is also one of the easiest to overlook. Communication is often strongest before a gift is made. The need is clear. The urgency is expressed. The invitation is carefully constructed. And then, once the donor responds, the communication slows.

The message, whether intended or not, is clear.

The relationship peaks at the point of giving.

But what if the opposite were true? What if the communication after the gift were just as thoughtful, just as clear, just as intentional as what came before? What if the donor's experience improved after they gave, rather than diminishing?

This becomes even more important in work that unfolds over time, like basic research. The outcomes are not immediate. The progress is not always visible. Which makes follow-through more difficult–and more necessary. You may not be able to point to a finished result, but you can show movement. What has been learned. What is being pursued next. Where the work is going.

Without that, silence fills the space.

And silence creates uncertainty. Not immediately, but over time. Did anything happen? Does this still matter? When there is no communication, the donor answers those questions on their own. And often, the answer leans toward doubt.

This is why stewardship requires intention. A rhythm. Not sporadic communication, but a structure. An acknowledgment that arrives promptly. A follow-up that connects the gift to the work. Ongoing updates that show progress. Future invitations that build on what has already been established.

Not a series of disconnected moments.

A relationship.

A useful question can bring this into focus. If you were the donor, what would you experience after giving? Not what is intended. Not what is assumed. What actually happens. If the answer feels thin, the relationship likely is as well.

The principle here is simple, but it changes everything that follows. The gift is not the end of the relationship. It is the beginning of the next one.

And how that beginning is handled shapes everything that comes after.

Because people remember how they are treated once they act. Whether their effort was noticed. Whether their contribution was valued. Whether their decision was reinforced. These are not large gestures. They are small, consistent signals. But over time, they accumulate.

Into trust.

Into loyalty.

Into the kind of relationship that does not need to be rebuilt each time you ask.

In the next chapter, the focus shifts again. To what happens when that trust begins to look for evidence. Not just reassurance, but proof.

Because once trust is given, it does not remain idle.

It looks for confirmation.

CHAPTER FIFTEEN

Proof Is the Promise Kept

Showing That What You Said Would Matter... Did

Every appeal, whether it states it plainly or not, makes a promise.

It may not appear in bold language. It may not be written out in full. But it is there, quietly shaping the exchange: if you do this, something will change.

That is the agreement.

The donor steps forward. They act. And in return, they expect—not immediately, not perfectly, but eventually—to see some evidence that their action mattered.

Before the gift, belief is borrowed. The donor trusts what you tell them. They trust your explanation, your intention, your credibility. But after the gift, something shifts. Belief no longer rests on what is said. It begins to depend on what can be seen.

Not everything. But something.

Without that, the promise begins to weaken.

The absence of proof does not create a dramatic break. There is no clear moment when trust disappears. Instead, the change is gradual. Uncertainty begins to creep in. Confidence softens. Future decisions feel less certain. Not because the work failed, but because the connection between the donor's action and the outcome was never made visible.

This is where many organizations misunderstand what proof actually is. It is not simply data. It is not a report filled with numbers or a summary of activity. Proof answers a simpler, more direct question: what happened because of this?

And just as important, how does that connect to what I did?

Organizations often report activity. Programs delivered. Hours completed. Initiatives launched. All of it real. All of it necessary. But activity describes effort. Proof describes effect.

The difference matters.

Saying that research initiatives were conducted over the past year tells you something happened. Saying that, because of support, that research moved forward–bringing new understanding within reach–connects the action to meaning. One reports. The other completes the story.

To do this well requires translation. Taking technical outcomes, internal progress, complex findings, and shaping them into something that can be understood quickly and clearly. Not by reducing the truth, but by interpreting it. By making visible what would otherwise remain abstract.

There is often a temptation to include everything. To show the full scope, to provide complete transparency, to leave nothing out. But too much information can obscure what matters most. Proof should be focused, clear, and directly tied to the donor's action.

It is not enough to say that progress is being made. Or that the work is impactful. These are assertions. They tell the reader what to believe without showing them why. Proof lives in what changed, what was learned, what is now possible that was not before.

This becomes more difficult in fields like basic research, where outcomes are not immediate or easily visible. There may be no cure to point to, no breakthrough that transforms everything overnight. But proof still exists. It lives in the steps forward. In questions answered. In new understanding. In movement toward something not yet complete.

You do not have to wait for the finish line to show progress. You can show that something is now understood that was not before. That a discovery has opened the door to the next phase of work. These are not endpoints, but they are not nothing. They are movement. And movement matters.

There is, however, a tension here. Donors often think in shorter timeframes than the work itself. They want to see that something is happening. The work, particularly in research, unfolds slowly. The answer is not to rush the work. It is to communicate progress in a way that keeps that forward motion visible.

Proof is not only intellectual. It is emotional. It reinforces the original decision. It allows the donor to feel, quietly but clearly, that they were right to act. Without that reinforcement, the experience remains incomplete.

A common failure follows from this. Organizations invest care and attention into the ask, shaping the message, refining the language, making the case. And then, after the gift, the communication becomes thinner. Less intentional. As though the outcome will speak for itself.

It rarely does.

Because outcomes, without context, remain distant. They need to be connected back to the donor, to the action that made them possible. The loop must be completed. You asked. They gave. Something happened. And that something must be visible, understandable, and clearly tied to what they chose to do.

A simple test can bring this into focus. If you were the donor, would you clearly see what your gift helped make possible? Not in general terms, but specifically. If the answer is uncertain, the proof is not yet complete.

Proof is not a single moment. It is a pattern. An initial update. Continued progress. Eventual outcomes. Each builds on the last. Each reinforces the relationship. Each strengthens trust.

Because that is what is at stake here.

Proof is not optional. It is the promise, kept and shown. Without it, trust begins to stall. With it, trust grows.

A donor gives based on belief. They continue giving based on experience. Proof is what transforms one into the other. It takes something that was hoped for and makes it visible. Not always complete. Not always final. But real enough to say: this moved forward.

And when that happens, the next decision becomes easier. Not because you ask again, but because the last answer still holds.

In the next chapter, the focus turns to something that seems simple, but is rarely done well. Gratitude—not as a formality, but as a continuation of the relationship.

CHAPTER SIXTEEN

Gratitude That Isn't Transactional

Thank You" Is Where the Relationship Either Deepens… or Drifts

There is a moment, just after a gift is made, when something delicate lingers.

The decision has only just settled. The action is still fresh. For a brief window, the donor is paying closer attention than they usually do—not to your organization, exactly, but to the meaning of what they've just chosen to do.

That moment does not last long. But it matters.

What you do next begins to define it.

Most organizations respond efficiently. The acknowledgment is sent. The receipt is issued. The system updates. Everything is completed correctly, and nothing is technically missing. But completion is not the same as connection.

A form email can confirm that a gift was received. It cannot confirm that it mattered.

This is where the tone of gratitude begins to shape the experience. Transactional gratitude sounds familiar. Thank you for your generous donation. It is accurate. It is appropriate. It is also interchangeable. It could come from anywhere, addressed to anyone. It closes the loop neatly, but it does not leave anything behind.

Real gratitude does something else.

It recognizes the decision that was made. It connects that decision to meaning. It reflects it back to the donor in a way that makes the action visible. It answers the question that is sitting quietly beneath the surface: did this matter?

After giving, donors are not wondering whether the gift was received. They assume that. What they are trying to understand is whether their choice had weight—whether it changed something, however small, in the direction of the work.

The difference between these two approaches is often subtle in language, but not in effect. Thank you for your support acknowledges the act. Because of you, this work moves forward connects the act to consequence. One confirms. The other affirms.

Specificity strengthens that connection. General gratitude fades quickly. Specific gratitude lingers. It names what the gift supports, what it enables, what shifts because of it. These details do not need to be extensive. They need to be clear enough that the donor can see where they stand inside the outcome.

Timing matters as well. Gratitude is most effective when it is close to the moment of giving. When the decision is still present, still alive. Delay does not erase the impact, but it weakens the connection. The further the response moves from the action, the less it reinforces it.

Systems make this easier, but they also introduce risk. Automation ensures that no one is missed. It reduces delay. It creates consistency. But if every message feels identical, the donor begins to feel the same way—interchangeable, processed, part of a system rather than part of something meaningful.

Automation is not the problem. Unshaped automation is.

Even within a system, the tone can remain human. The message can remain intentional. The connection can still be felt.

And gratitude does not end with the first message.

It continues in quieter ways. A follow-up note. A brief update. A small acknowledgment that arrives without an ask attached. These are not required, and precisely for that reason, they are remembered. They signal that the relationship did not end at the point of giving.

This becomes especially important in work like basic research, where outcomes do not arrive quickly. You cannot say that a gift solved the problem or produced an immediate result. But you can say that it moved the work forward. And over time, you can show what that movement looks like.

In this context, gratitude becomes part of the story itself. Not a closing line, but an opening into what comes next.

The risk, as always, is that gratitude becomes routine. Another step in the process. Something to complete and move past. When that happens, it loses its force–not because the words change, but because the intention behind them does.

It helps to return to the moment itself. Each gift is not a metric. Not a number in a report. It is a decision. A person chose to act. That choice deserves more than a standard response. It deserves to be recognized for what it is.

A simple test can make this clear. Read your thank-you message and ask whether it would feel meaningful if you received it. Not acceptable. Not correct. Meaningful. If it does not, it needs to be reconsidered.

Because gratitude shapes memory. It influences how the donor remembers giving, how they feel about the organization, whether they choose to return. It is not separate from fundraising. It is part of it.

The principle underneath it is straightforward. Gratitude is not the end of the interaction. It is the beginning of the next one.

A thank-you can function as a formality. Or it can act as a signal–that the decision was seen, the action was valued, and the connection matters. One closes the loop.

The other keeps it open.

And in this work, things do not continue because the loop was closed efficiently.

They continue because it was left open in the right way.

In the next chapter, the focus shifts to a moment many find more difficult than any other–the ask itself. Not something to soften or avoid, but something to make clear, direct, and worthy of the decision it invites.

CHAPTER SEVENTEEN

Asking Is an Act of Respect

Clarity at the Moment of Decision Matters More Than Comfort

There is a point in every piece of fundraising where everything gathers.

The story has done its work. The stakes have taken shape. The meaning has settled into place. What began as explanation has become something closer to recognition.

And then the moment arrives. Something has to happen.

You have to ask.

This is where the tone often shifts, almost imperceptibly. Not in the structure of the message, but in the confidence behind it. The language softens. The edges blur. The ask begins to step back from itself, as though hoping the reader will arrive at it without it needing to be stated.

We hope you'll consider. If you're able. Any support is appreciated.

The phrasing is polite. It is careful. It avoids pressure. It also avoids clarity.

The hesitation is easy to understand. No one wants to appear forceful. No one wants to create discomfort or risk overstepping. There is a quiet instinct to preserve goodwill, to let the donor decide without feeling directed.

But something is lost in that restraint.

Because by the time the ask arrives, the donor is no longer deciding whether they care. That question has already been answered. The message has done that work.

Now they are asking something else. What do I do?

If the answer is unclear, the moment stalls. And when a decision stalls, it often disappears.

There is a tendency to confuse directness with pressure. To assume that naming the action plainly somehow forces the outcome. But pressure tries to compel. Clarity simply shows the path.

Make a gift today to move this work forward.

There is nothing coercive in that sentence. It does not demand. It does not persuade through force. It identifies the step and leaves the decision where it belongs—with the donor.

When the ask is softened, ambiguity takes its place. Is this optional? Is this urgent? Is this expected? The donor is left to interpret, and interpretation introduces friction. Even small amounts of friction can be enough to interrupt action.

Clarity, in this moment, is not a matter of efficiency. It is a form of respect. It acknowledges that something matters, that the donor has a real role to play, and that it is worth stating that role plainly. It trusts them to decide, without manipulation and without evasion.

You can feel the difference in even the simplest shift. We invite you to consider supporting our efforts suggests a possibility. You can help move this research forward by making a gift today provides direction. One gestures. The other opens a door.

Hesitation in the ask often carries an unintended signal. It introduces doubt. Not overtly, but enough to be felt. If the organization seems uncertain, the donor senses it. Confidence, in this context, does not come from force. It comes from clarity.

A strong ask answers three questions, whether explicitly or not. What should I do? When should I do it? Why does it matter now? If any of these remain unclear, the ask weakens. Not dramatically, but enough to reduce the likelihood of action.

There is still room for flexibility. Clarity does not eliminate choice. It can coexist with it. Make a gift at a level that is meaningful to you offers space without removing direction. The path is still visible, even if the exact step varies.

This becomes even more important in work like basic research, where the outcome is not immediate or visible. The donor cannot point to a finished result. They are acting on belief. Which means the ask itself must carry more weight. It must connect clearly to what the action enables.

Help fund the next step in understanding how this disease begins.

Now the action has context. It has direction. It has meaning.

There is often a search for the perfect way to ask. The right phrasing, the ideal timing, the exact moment when everything aligns. So the language is refined, adjusted, softened, revisited. But the perfect moment rarely creates action. Clarity does.

When the ask is avoided or obscured, the message does not fail in obvious ways. It simply underperforms. Quietly. Repeatedly. Because people do not act on what is implied. They act on what is clear.

A useful test is simple. At the end of your message, ask whether someone would know exactly what to do next. Not generally. Not approximately. Exactly. If the answer is uncertain, the work is not finished.

A clear ask is not a demand. It is an invitation. It says, this matters, you can be part of it, here is how. Nothing more. Nothing less.

This is what resolves the tension around asking. Clarity is not pressure. It is respect. It gives the donor something real to respond to.

And when everything leading up to that moment is aligned—when the story is grounded, the stakes are clear, and the offer is meaningful—the ask does not feel like an interruption.

It feels like a natural continuation.

A simple point where someone is given the chance to act.

And all that remains is to make that moment clear enough for them to meet it.

Timing, Tone, and Tension
When and How You Ask Matters as Much as What You Say

A good message, delivered at the wrong moment, will underperform.

A clear ask, expressed in the wrong tone, will hesitate.

And a campaign that lacks tension—without a sense that something is at stake now—will drift. Not in a way that draws attention. Not in a way that clearly signals failure. It will simply fail to move.

Quietly.

This is because every ask is shaped by more than the message itself. Beneath the words are three forces that determine whether it lands or fades: timing, tone, and tension. Most organizations focus on what they are saying. These three determine whether it is heard.

Timing is the first of them, though it is often misunderstood. Messages do not arrive in isolation. They enter crowded days, divided attention, moments that were already in motion long before your message appeared. People are working, distracted, moving quickly from one thing to the next. Your message is not the center of that experience. It is an interruption within it.

There is a tendency to search for the perfect moment. The right day, the right season, the ideal alignment of conditions. These things matter, but not as much as they seem. There is rarely a perfect moment waiting to be found. There are only moments that are more or less aligned with someone's ability to receive what you are saying.

Timing, in that sense, is not about precision. It is about awareness. Whether the message arrives when there is space to notice it. Whether it follows something that has prepared the ground. Whether it appears as part of a sequence rather than standing alone.

Because one message, no matter how strong, is rarely enough.

People do not ignore messages because they are unwilling. They miss them because they are busy. Cadence creates the rhythm that allows a message to be seen more than once. An initial message, a follow-up, a reinforcement. Not repetition for its own sake, but repetition that deepens understanding.

There is often hesitation here. A concern that repeating a message will feel excessive, even intrusive. But repetition, when the message is clear and grounded, does not feel like noise. It feels like reinforcement.

Tone is the next force, and it operates more quickly than most realize. Before the words are fully processed, the reader has already formed an impression. How am I being spoken to?

Tone can drift without intention. It can lean toward urgency without grounding, politeness without clarity, confidence without warmth. Each carries its own risk. Urgency without grounding begins to feel exaggerated. Politeness without clarity feels hesitant. Confidence without warmth creates distance.

The balance is subtle, but it matters.

A strong tone does not raise its voice. It does not soften its meaning. It does not overstate its importance. It remains steady. Clear, calm, direct, and grounded in what is true.

You can hear the difference in even a small shift. Saying that support is urgently needed in a critical moment reaches for intensity. Saying that the work cannot move forward without support—and that now is the moment to act—creates the same sense of urgency, but with credibility intact.

Tension is the third force, and without it, nothing moves.

Not because people do not care. But because there is no reason to act now instead of later. Tension is not pressure. It is not urgency for its own sake, and it is not created by artificial deadlines. It comes from clarity—about timing, about consequence, about what is possible in this moment.

Something is at risk. Something is within reach. Something changes depending on whether action is taken now.

When that is clear, movement becomes possible.

When it is not, delay becomes the default.

There is a danger, however, in overstating urgency. If every message carries the same intensity, the same insistence that everything is critical, the language begins to lose its meaning. Not all at once, but gradually. Over time, donors learn to discount what they hear, and urgency becomes background noise.

Real tension does not need to be amplified. It needs to be revealed.

These three forces—timing, tone, and tension—do not operate independently. They interact. A message delivered at the right moment but with the wrong tone will falter. A message with strong tone but no tension will stall. A message with tension but poor timing may never be seen at all.

Alignment matters more than any single element.

Before sending a message, it is worth pausing to consider each of them. Whether the timing allows for attention. Whether the tone feels clear and grounded. Whether the reason to act now is visible and real. If any of these are missing, the message weakens—not dramatically, but enough to matter.

This becomes more complex in areas like basic research, where the work itself unfolds over long periods and outcomes are not immediate. The idea of "now" is harder to define. But it still exists. Now is when the work can move forward. Now is when a question can be pursued. Now is when delay can be avoided.

That is enough.

When these elements fall out of alignment, the effect is rarely obvious. The message is seen, but not felt. Read, but not acted on. Understood, but not urgent. And the moment passes.

What emerges from this is a simple principle: a message works when timing, tone, and tension align. Miss one, and the whole begins to shift.

Because the ask is not a single point on the page. It is a moment shaped by context–by how it arrives, how it sounds, and whether it gives someone a reason to act now.

Get those right, and the message finds its footing. Not because it is louder, but because it meets the moment it enters.

And once that moment passes, the work does not end.

In the next chapter, the focus moves to what follows. Not the first gift, but the second.

Because the first decision is an introduction.

The second is something else entirely.

The Second Gift Is the Real Test

Why Retention Reveals What the First Gift Conceals

The first gift feels like success.

It arrives. It confirms interest. It suggests that something worked. For a moment, that is enough. The effort led somewhere. The message reached someone. A decision was made.

And yet, the first gift answers only a limited question.

Did this message move someone once?

The second gift answers something far more important.

Did the experience hold?

There is a quiet illusion that settles around the first gift. It begins to feel like a milestone, a conversion, a completed effort. A point you have reached. But it is better understood as something else entirely.

An introduction.

A beginning.

A moment when someone says, "I am willing to try this."

Not, "I am committed."

That distinction matters more than it appears.

Because the first gift is shaped by many things that are not stable. Timing. Emotion. Context. The strength of a single message. It can happen quickly. It can happen impulsively. It can happen without depth. Which makes it a poor measure of trust on its own.

The second gift is different.

It requires memory. Reflection. Continued belief. It asks the donor, quietly but directly, whether the experience was worth repeating. Not whether the message was persuasive, but whether the experience itself held together over time.

Between those two moments—between the first gift and the second—many relationships begin to thin.

Not because the first interaction failed.

Because what followed it did not sustain it.

The connection weakens. The communication becomes less intentional. The meaning that once felt clear begins to fade. And when the next ask arrives, it feels more distant, less compelling, easier to decline.

This is the space where continuity matters.

Something has to hold between those two decisions. Not constantly, but consistently. Reminders of the work. Evidence that something has moved forward. Signals that the relationship did not end at the moment of giving.

Without that, the donor is left to reconstruct the connection from memory alone.

And memory, without reinforcement, fades.

What remains after a gift is not just the transaction, but a kind of emotional residue. A feeling that lingers. It may be satisfaction. It may be uncertainty. It may be a sense of connection, or a quiet doubt. What you do after the gift shapes that feeling. And that feeling shapes the next decision.

There is a familiar pattern that works against this. Organizations invest heavily in acquisition. The messaging is strong. The ask is clear. The outreach is effective. The first gift arrives.

And then the focus shifts.

To new audiences. New campaigns. New goals.

The donor who just gave becomes one among many, part of a broader list, less central to the effort than they were just moments before. And slowly, almost invisibly, retention begins to erode.

This is often treated as an efficiency problem.

It is not.

It is a trust problem.

A second gift carries meaning that the first does not. It says, I remember. I believe. I am willing to continue. It reflects something deeper than a single response. It reflects an experience that held together long enough to invite repetition.

Replacing that is costly.

Not just in resources, but in effort. Each new donor requires the work to begin again—to introduce, to explain, to connect. Retention builds on what already exists. It carries something forward instead of starting over.

The path from one gift to the next is not complicated.

It is consistent.

A clear acknowledgment. A follow-up that connects the gift to meaning. Ongoing signals of progress. A return to the donor before the next ask arrives. Each step reinforces the last. Each keeps the relationship active.

When the second ask comes, it should not feel like a reset. It should feel like a continuation. Because you helped begin this, here is what has moved forward—and here is what comes next.

Now the donor is not being asked to start over.

They are being invited to continue.

Even the language shifts. The first gift is an invitation to join. The second is an invitation to continue what has already begun. The difference is small, but it changes the experience entirely.

Because after the first gift, the donor is no longer an observer. They are no longer a prospect. They are someone who has acted. And your communication should recognize that—not as flattery, but as fact.

When the second ask feels identical to the first, something is lost. The relationship has not progressed. It has remained static. And static relationships rarely deepen.

But when the second gift happens, something changes.

It becomes easier to stay connected. Easier to give again. Easier to increase commitment. Not automatically, but more naturally. Because the foundation is stronger.

This is the shift worth paying attention to.

The first gift is a response.

The second gift is a decision.

And it is the second that begins to define the relationship.

The first gift carries hope. It suggests possibility. The second confirms that the possibility held. That the experience was real enough, meaningful enough, clear enough to return to.

And in that return, something begins to take shape.

Not just support.

But relationship.

In the next chapter, we step back from these individual moments and look at how they connect—how each piece, when aligned, forms something that can move, hold, and build over time.

CHAPTER NINETEEN
The Bridge Model
How It All Fits Together When It Finally Starts to Work

Up to this point, the work has been taken apart.

Piece by piece, each element examined on its own terms. The role of the donor. The structure of the story. The function of emotion. The necessity of clarity. The discipline of systems. The importance of trust. Each of these matters. Each can be understood independently. Each can be improved.

And yet, none of them operate alone.

This is where many organizations encounter a quiet frustration. They improve one part of the process. The messaging becomes stronger. The ask becomes clearer. The follow-up becomes more intentional. And still, the results feel uneven. Progress appears, then slips. Gains are made, then lost.

Because improvement in isolation does not guarantee movement.

These elements are not separate pieces. They are connected parts of a single structure. And when one part shifts without the others, the whole does not necessarily strengthen.

To understand what is happening, you have to step back. Not into abstraction, but into structure. You have to see how the parts move together. Where they support each other. Where they fail each other. Where the connection breaks, even when the individual pieces seem sound.

It helps to think of this work as a bridge.

Not as a metaphor for appearance, but as a structure with a purpose. It carries someone across a distance–from awareness, to understanding, to action, to continued engagement. It is not decorative. It is functional. It either holds, or it does not.

And when it does not, the failure is rarely in a single beam.

The bridge is made of connected elements, each leading to the next. A story that can be understood. Emotion that makes it felt. Trust that allows it to be believed. An action that can be taken. Proof that something happened because of it. Continuation that carries the relationship forward.

Each step prepares the next. Not perfectly, but predictably.

Most failures do not occur within these elements themselves. They occur at the points where one is meant to lead into another. The message may be clear, but nothing moves because it is not felt. The emotion may be present, but trust is not strong enough to support action. The ask may succeed, but the absence of proof weakens what follows. The first gift may arrive, but without continuation, the relationship thins.

The structure is only as strong as its connections.

When something underperforms, the instinct is often to change everything. Rewrite the message. Adjust the strategy. Shift the approach entirely. But this is rarely necessary. A more useful question is simpler.

Where is the break?

If people are not engaging, the story or the emotional connection may not be holding. If they engage but do not act, the issue may lie in trust or in the clarity of the ask. If they give once but do not return, the breakdown is likely in proof or in continuation.

This narrows the work. It makes improvement specific instead of general. It turns uncertainty into something that can be addressed.

Order matters here as well.

You cannot ask before meaning is clear. You cannot prove something before action has taken place. You cannot build trust after it has already been weakened. Each step prepares the ground for the next. Skipping ahead does not accelerate the process. It destabilizes it.

Follow the path from the beginning, and the structure becomes visible. A story introduces the work. Emotion gives it weight. Trust makes it credible. The ask invites action. Proof shows that the action mattered. Continuation carries the relationship forward.

When these align, movement occurs.

Not always dramatically. But consistently.

And consistency is what turns isolated success into something reliable.

Because the bridge is not built once.

It is maintained.

Each campaign reinforces it or strains it. Each interaction strengthens it or weakens it. Over time, it becomes something people recognize, something they trust, something they are willing to cross again. Or it does not.

Fragmentation is what breaks it.

When messaging is disconnected from follow-up, when the ask is disconnected from proof, when gratitude is disconnected from meaning, each part may function on its own. But the whole begins to fail. The experience becomes uneven. The path becomes unclear.

Alignment is what holds it together.

Not perfection. Not uniformity. But coherence. The message matches the ask. The ask connects to the outcome. The outcome is communicated back clearly. Each part supports the next.

This becomes even more important in complex work like basic research, where the timelines are longer, the outcomes less visible, and the uncertainty greater. Without structure, the message fragments. It becomes inconsistent, uneven, difficult to follow.

With structure, it holds.

The story clarifies what is happening. Emotion connects it to meaning. Trust supports belief in the process. Proof shows movement, even when results are still emerging. The bridge remains intact, even when the destination is not yet fully visible.

A simple test can reveal whether that structure is working.

If someone enters at the beginning, can they move all the way through? Not just to understand or feel, but to act, to see what happened, to continue the relationship.

If any part of that path is unclear, the bridge needs reinforcement.

This is what ties everything together.

The work succeeds when each part leads naturally to the next. Not by force. By design.

Because philanthropy is not a single moment. It is not an isolated decision.

It is a movement.

From awareness to meaning. From meaning to action. From action to trust. From trust to continuation.

The bridge is what carries that movement.

Not perfectly. But reliably.

And when it holds, something changes.

People do not simply respond once.

They return.

They continue.

They become part of something that extends beyond a single decision.

And that is where the work begins to sustain itself.

Chapter Twenty

Corporate Giving
Clarity in a structured environment

Corporate philanthropy rarely feels like a person when you first encounter it.

It arrives as a system.

Budgets, priorities, timelines, approval chains. Language that sounds measured. Decisions that appear orderly, even distant. It carries the weight of an institution, and it is easy–almost automatic–to assume that it operates by a different set of rules.

That this is purely strategic work.

That if you align correctly, match the right priorities, use the right phrases, the decision will follow.

For a while, that assumption seems to hold.

Until you stay close to it long enough to notice something quieter underneath.

Inside the structure, there are still people.

Someone reading. Someone weighing. Someone deciding whether this belongs here, in this organization, at this moment. Someone who will need to explain that decision, justify it, and stand behind it once it is made.

The system shapes the process.

It does not replace the decision.

And that is where the work often begins to drift.

Organizations start writing to the structure instead of through it. They adjust their language until it fits perfectly within corporate priorities. They mirror what they believe is expected. They align so completely that the message becomes smooth, polished–and indistinct.

It fits. But it does not hold.

Because alignment, on its own, is not enough.

When everything sounds right, nothing stands out. When every proposal feels interchangeable, every decision becomes easier to defer. The work begins to disappear into the very system it was meant to navigate.

There is a quieter, stronger position available.

This is what we do.

This is why it matters.

And here is where it meets what you care about.

It does not try to become something else.

It stays itself—and allows alignment to emerge where it is real.

And real alignment carries weight that imitation never does.

Because beneath the process, the same questions remain.

Why this?

Why now?

Why here?

Those are not answered by compliance. They are answered by clarity, by relevance, and by belief.

This is where the next tension appears.

Corporations ask about outcomes. They have to. They need to understand what will change, what can be measured, what can be reported.

And in response, organizations often begin to stretch.

They promise more than they should. They push toward certainty. They try to make the work sound finished before it is.

But credibility is the quiet currency in this space.

And once it weakens, it is difficult to rebuild.

The stronger approach is not to inflate. It is to clarify.

What moves forward?

What becomes possible?

What changes because this work continues?

In basic research, this matters even more. There is no immediate resolution. No finished answer to point to. What you are offering is not a cure, but movement toward one.

That is not a limitation.

It is the truth.

And truth, stated plainly, holds longer than certainty that cannot be sustained.

There is another layer that often goes unnoticed.

Corporate philanthropy always has two audiences.

The one outside; the communities, the public, the stakeholders who will see the work.

And the one inside–the people who must approve it, explain it, and continue to support it.

A message that leans too far in either direction begins to weaken.

Too transactional, and it loses meaning.

Too emotional, and it loses footing.

The balance is not complicated.

It is simply clear.

This matters.

This aligns.

This works.

That is enough.

There is also a persistent belief that scale carries the decision.

That larger numbers, broader reach, bigger claims will make the case more compelling.

Scale has its place.

But it does not come first.

Clarity does.

An organization cannot support what it cannot see. A single, specific outcome–something that can be understood, pictured, explained–often carries more weight than a page of abstract reach.

From that point, scale can expand.

But it does not begin there.

And beneath all of it, something else matters more than the process itself.

The relationship.

It is easy to treat corporate philanthropy as a transaction. A proposal submitted. A grant awarded. A report delivered.

Completed.

But that repeats a familiar mistake.

Because inside every corporate decision, there is someone who said yes.

Someone who read the work, made the case, connected it internally, and chose to move it forward.

That person matters more than the process that surrounds them.

They are the bridge.

And your work, in part, is to make their decision hold. To make it clear, defensible, and meaningful–not as strategy alone, but as recognition of what they chose to do.

This is where follow-through takes its full weight.

Reports are expected. That is part of the structure. But what is actually being evaluated goes beyond the report.

Did this move the work?

Was this the right decision?

Would we do this again?

Those answers are not found in data alone.

They are found in connection.

In how clearly outcomes are tied back to the original decision. In how consistently the relationship is maintained. In whether the work remains visible after the moment of giving has passed.

In the end, corporate philanthropy does not require a different philosophy.

It requires the same one, applied with discipline inside a more structured environment.

Clarity still matters.

Emotion still begins the response.

Trust still sustains it.

Proof still reinforces it.

And continuation still determines what comes next.

The structure may be more complex. The language more measured. The process more layered.

But the movement is unchanged.

Something is presented.

A decision is made.

Support is given.

And something begins to move forward that would not have moved without it.

Your task is not simply to navigate the structure.

It is to make the meaning clear enough that the structure supports the decision–rather than replaces it.

Because even here, at scale, inside systems that appear impersonal, the work still comes down to the same moment it always has.

Someone reads.

Pauses.

And decides.

Yes.

This is worth doing.

In the next chapter, the lens shifts again–away from structure and into practice. What this looks like when it meets the real world, where the work is not theoretical, but lived, tested, and refined over time.

Chapter Twenty One

What This Looks Like in the Wild
How Theory Behaves Once It Leaves the Building

It is one thing to understand the pieces.

It is another to watch them work together when the conditions are less forgiving. When deadlines press. When priorities compete. When attention is limited and time is shorter than you would like. This is where ideas stop being theoretical. This is where they are tested.

Not in clean outlines.

In real conditions.

Most organizations, if they are honest about it, know more than they apply. They understand the importance of clarity. They recognize the role of the donor. They can describe the need for emotion, for trust, for structure. The principles are not unfamiliar.

And yet, when the work begins, something shifts.

Messages begin to stretch. They grow longer. Focus drifts inward. The organization edges back toward the center of the story. The ask softens, just slightly, enough to introduce hesitation.

Not because the ideas are unclear.

Because execution is harder than understanding.

To see how this plays out, it helps to walk through the work as it actually happens. Not in a perfect version, but in one that reflects reality.

The starting point often sounds something like this: a careful description of the work, accurate and well-formed, filled with the right language. It explains what is happening, outlines the scope, conveys seriousness. It is, in many ways, correct.

And yet it remains distant.

So the first shift is toward clarity. The message is reworked until it can be understood quickly, without effort. The work takes shape. It becomes something a reader can grasp in a single pass.

Then comes emotion. Not added as decoration, but drawn out of what is already true. A moment is introduced. A change that can be seen. Not exaggerated, not overstated–just made visible. Now the message is not only understood. It is felt.

From there, the donor enters. Not as an observer, but as someone who can act. The message opens a role, something specific enough to recognize. A place within the outcome.

Then the ask is made. Clearly. Directly. Without hesitation. Not as pressure, but as direction.

And after the action, the work continues. The follow-through connects the gift to what has happened because of it. The promise is carried forward into something visible.

The work itself has not changed.

The science is the same. The mission is the same. What has changed is the structure. And that structure determines whether the message moves someone or simply informs them.

Even with this understanding, the process is not stable by default. It can falter in small ways that are easy to miss.

Clarity gives way to complexity as more is added than necessary. The organization, almost by habit, returns to the center. The follow-through becomes thinner than the ask that preceded it. Each shift is minor. The accumulation is not.

This is where discipline matters.

Not as rigidity, but as consistency. Returning to the same questions, each time. Is this clear? Is the donor inside the story? Is the ask direct? Is the outcome visible? Not asked once, but asked repeatedly.

When something underperforms, the instinct is often to begin again. To replace the message, to change direction, to look for something entirely new. But more often, the work does not need to be reinvented. It needs to be adjusted. The story clarified. The stakes sharpened. The ask made more direct.

Small changes, applied consistently, do more than constant reinvention.

Because the work rarely happens under ideal conditions. It happens within constraints. Limited time. Competing demands. Incomplete information. The goal is not to remove those constraints. It is to work within them. To achieve enough clarity, enough structure, enough consistency to move forward.

A simple check can help anchor this. Before a campaign is sent, step back and ask whether it can be understood quickly. Whether there is something to feel. Whether the donor can see their place in the outcome. Whether the ask is clear. Whether there is a plan for what follows.

If any of these are uncertain, the message is not yet ready.

Over time, something begins to shift.

Not suddenly. Not dramatically. But steadily. Messages become clearer. Responses become more consistent. Relationships begin to hold. Not because of a single breakthrough, but because of repeated alignment.

Even then, not everything will succeed. Some efforts will fall short. Some campaigns will underperform. Some messages will not land as expected. This is not a failure of the system. It is part of the work.

The goal is not perfection.

It is progress.

And progress depends on what happens next. After each effort, the work returns to the structure. Where did it hold? Where did it weaken? What can be improved, specifically, next time? Not in general terms, but in clear, practical ones.

Because understanding the work is not enough.

Doing it—consistently, under real conditions—is what produces results.

Ideas behave differently in the real world. They encounter time constraints, competing priorities, imperfect execution. And they either hold, or they don't.

Your work is to make them hold.

Not through complexity. Not through constant change.

But through clear, consistent application.

Over time.

And in the final chapter, the focus shifts one last time. Not to introduce something new, but to step back and see what remains when everything else is stripped away. What this work ultimately asks of you—and what it gives in return.

Chapter Twenty Two

A Few Things Learned the Hard Way

What Remains After the Campaign Ends and the Numbers Settle

If you stay in this work long enough, patterns begin to repeat.

Not because the field stands still. It doesn't. New tools arrive. New platforms take hold. Language shifts, strategies evolve, approaches cycle in and out of favor. On the surface, it looks like constant change.

But underneath that movement, something else persists.

People.

And people do not change as quickly as the tools designed to reach them.

So the same lessons return. Quietly. Consistently. Usually not when things are going well, but when something has gone wrong. When a campaign underperforms. When a message fails to land. When results do not match effort.

That is when the work teaches you.

The first lesson is often the hardest to accept. Good work is not enough.

The mission can be real. The need can be undeniable. The effort can be sincere and substantial. And still, none of that guarantees support. Not because the work lacks value, but because value that is not clearly seen might as well not exist. You can do meaningful work and fail to move anyone to act if that work is not made visible in a way people can understand.

The second lesson follows quickly behind it. If you confuse, you lose.

Confusion rarely announces itself. It does not provoke argument or resistance. It simply causes people to move on. A message that is unclear, overly complex, or difficult to follow does not get debated. It gets left behind. Clarity is not a refinement. It is a requirement.

Over time, another shift can happen if you are not careful. Donors begin to look like categories. Segments. Targets. Audiences to be managed. It is efficient. It is measurable. It is also where something important begins to slip.

Because people are not problems to solve.

They are participants.

And they can tell when they are being treated as one or the other.

There is also a tendency, especially as the work becomes more sophisticated, to believe that better results require more complexity. More detail. More nuance. More layers of explanation. But again and again, something simpler proves more effective.

Clear. Direct. Focused.

Not because simplicity is easier, but because it is harder to ignore.

Trust, meanwhile, builds in ways that are easy to overlook. Not in large gestures, but in accumulation. One message. One interaction. One promise kept. Over time, it becomes something steady. And just as quietly, it can weaken. A missed follow-up. An unclear message. A connection that is implied but never shown. You rarely notice the moment it shifts. But eventually, you feel the result.

The first "yes" a donor gives is not the end of anything. It is a beginning.

It is tentative. Open. Conditional in ways that are not spoken aloud. What happens after that first decision determines what comes next. Whether they return. Whether they deepen their support. Whether the relationship continues at all. The second decision is always harder. And always more revealing.

There are parts of this work that can be handed off. Design. Distribution. Execution. Entire systems can be built to support those pieces.

But meaning cannot be outsourced.

It has to be understood, translated, and carried through the work with intention. No tool will do that for you. No system will replace it. It is the part that remains human, no matter how much else changes.

And there is something else worth acknowledging.

Not everything that works will feel comfortable.

Being direct in the ask can feel too forward. Simplifying complex ideas can feel like leaving something important behind. Focusing on one story instead of many can feel incomplete. But discomfort is not always a warning. Sometimes it is a sign that you are moving away from habit and toward something more effective.

Over time, another pattern becomes clear. Intensity produces results in bursts. A strong campaign, a concentrated effort, a moment where everything aligns.

But consistency produces something else.

Stability.

Clearer messaging. Stronger relationships. More reliable outcomes. Not because any one effort is perfect, but because the work is aligned often enough to hold.

And here is the part that surprises most people.

You are likely closer than you think.

Most organizations do not need to begin again. They do not need a complete reinvention or a radically new approach. What they need is refinement. Clearer language. Stronger structure. More consistent follow-through. The distance between where they are and where they want to be is often smaller than it appears.

Beneath all of this sits something even simpler.

Hope.

Not the kind that waits. Not the kind that sits in the corner with their fingers crossed and politely wishes. But the kind that acts. That decides. That steps forward with a fierce resilience and takes part in what could be, rather than standing back from it.

That is what this work is really about.

Everything else—the messaging, the structure, the systems—exists to support a single exchange.

This matters.

You can be part of it.

Here is how.

And someone else, somewhere, decides.

Yes. I will.

If there is one idea that carries through all of it, it is this: make it clear, make it meaningful, make it real. Not once, but consistently. Not perfectly, but deliberately.

Because this work does not depend on getting everything exactly right.

It depends on alignment.

On the quiet discipline of bringing three things into the same line: what you are doing, how you explain it, and how it is experienced by someone encountering it for the first time. Most of the time, those things sit slightly apart. The work is there. The explanation is close. The experience is something else entirely.

But when they come together, something begins to shift.

Not dramatically. Not all at once. But steadily.

People begin to see the work for what it is. They understand it without effort. And more importantly, they recognize where they fit within it.

That is when they step in.

And when they do, the effect does not remain contained. It moves outward—into the work, into the lives it touches, into outcomes that would not have existed otherwise.

Not because everything was perfect.

Because everything aligned.

The campaigns will change. The tools will evolve. The language will continue to shift.

But this remains.

Clear meaning. Honest connection. Work that matters, made visible.

And if you hold to that, over time, you will find that what you are building is not just support.

It is something steadier.

Something that lasts.

Something that, when done well, begins to resemble what it always was meant to be.

Hope– with its sleeves rolled up.

Bibliography

Ahern, T. (2012). *How to write fundraising materials that raise more money: The art, the science, the secrets.* Emerson & Church.

Buchanan, P. (2019). *Giving done right: Effective philanthropy and making every dollar count.* PublicAffairs.

Burk, P. (2003). *Donor-centered fundraising.* Cygnus Applied Research.

Cialdini, R. B. (2006). *Influence: The psychology of persuasion* (Rev. ed.). Harper Business

Donnelly, M., Karibi-Whyte, R., & Tarasov, O. (2011). *A Framework for Optimizing Institutional Effectiveness and Impact.* McKinsey & Company/Rockefeller Philanthropy Advisors

Frumkin, P. (2006). *Strategic giving: The art and science of philanthropy.* University of Chicago Press.

Godin, S. (2008). *Tribes: We need you to lead us.* Portfolio.

Godin, S. (2018). *This is marketing: You can't be seen until you learn to see.* Portfolio.

Gould, J. (2009). *Fundraising principles and practice.* Jossey-Bass.

Heath, C., & Heath, D. (2007). *Made to stick: Why some ideas survive and others die.* Random House.

Kahneman, D. (2011). *Thinking, fast and slow.* Farrar, Straus and Giroux.

MacKenzie, S. (2017). *Fundraising 401: Master classes in nonprofit fundraising.* Jossey-Bass.

Miller, K. L. (2010). *The nonprofit marketing guide: High-impact, low-cost ways to build support for your good cause.* Jossey-Bass.

Morino, M. (2011). *Leap of reason: Managing to outcomes in an era of scarcity.* Venture Philanthropy Partners.

Panas, J. (2006). *Asking: A 59-minute guide to everything board members, volunteers, and staff must know to secure the gift.* Emerson & Church.

Panas, J. (2007). *Mega gifts: Who gives them, who gets them.* Emerson & Church.

Pink, D. H. (2009). *Drive: The surprising truth about what motivates us.* Riverhead Books.

Rosen, M. J. (2012). *Donor-centered planned gift marketing.* Wiley.

Sargeant, A., & Shang, J. (2010). *Fundraising principles and practice.* Jossey-Bass.

Tierney, T. J., & Fleishman, J. L. (2011). *Give smart: Philanthropy that gets results.* PublicAffairs.

About the Author

Mark Donnelly, PhD is the graybeard lecturer who turned a squeaky whiteboard and a well-traveled tweed sport coat into a teaching philosophy.

A former marketing professor, brand consultant, author of more than sixty books, historian, photographer, and creative instigator, he has spent decades making complex ideas feel simple–and making people wonder if it's all that coffee, or if he's naturally this intense.

Dr. Donnelly built his reputation the old-fashioned way: by simplifying the truth. Not the polished, buzzword-heavy version, but the kind that holds up after watching trends rise, fall. With more than thirty years in academia, his work has also moved through newspapers, publishing, consulting, community initiatives, and philanthropic strategy–collecting stories, experience, and more old books than any one person needs.

At the center of his work is a single question: how do you make important work visible in a way that invites others to take part in it? That question has shaped his approach across education, communication, and non-profit philanthropy, especially in areas where clarity matters and certainty is rare.

His philosophy is simple: philanthropy is not persuasion–it is participation. Donors are not audiences–they are actors.

Dr. Donnelly lives and creates in Buffalo with his bride, Princess Laura, surrounded by notebooks and half-finished ideas. His guiding principle remains unchanged:

Make a difference.

This book is his latest attempt to do exactly that.

Other Timeless Books in the Graybeard Lectures Series:

Each stands alone.

Together, they form a unique, common sense curriculum.

Graybeard Lectures: Marketing

Drawn from smudged whiteboards and lived experience, This book cuts through buzzwords and trends to reveal how branding, storytelling, word of mouth, and purpose actually work–by understanding humans first. Warm, humorous, and practical, it's a guide for anyone who wants marketing that makes sense and lasts.

Graybeard Lectures: Branding

Branding is not decoration. It's definition.This book challenges the modern habit of treating brands as visual projects instead of behavioral ones. Logos matter less than promises kept. Consistency matters more than cleverness. Reputation is built slowly and lost quickly.

Graybeard Lectures: Advertising

Advertising doesn't fail because people stopped paying attention. It fails because it forgets how attention works.

This book explores why the most effective advertising aligns with human instincts rather than fighting them. It examines timing, context, repetition, and emotional truth without chasing trends or tactics.

Graybeard Lectures: Market Research

Listening Past The Numbers is a clear-eyed look at why market research often delivers confidence instead of understanding. It challenges the misuse of data, dashboards, and statistics, arguing for research grounded in human behavior, context, and judgment. Rather than offering tools, the book offers a wiser way to think, listen, and decide when the numbers start acting certain.

www.ingramcontent.com/pod-product-compliance
Lightning Source LLC
Chambersburg PA
CBHW040452240726
48664CB00008B/1634